Whole Language Strategies
for Secondary Students

Whole Language Strategies for Secondary Students

Edited by **Carol Gilles, Mary Bixby, Paul Crowley, Shirley R. Crenshaw, Margaret Henrichs, Frances E. Reynolds, Donelle Pyle**

With an Introduction and Theoretical Chapter by

Dorothy J. Watson

Richard C. Owen Publishers, Inc.
New York

Library of Congress Cataloging-in-Publication Data

Watson, Dorothy J. (Dorothy Jo), 1930–
    Whole language strategies for secondary students.

    Bibliography: p.
    Includes Index.
    1. Language arts (Secondary)   2. Reading—Language
experience approach.   3. Language arts—Correlation with
content subjects.   4. Interdisciplinary approach in
education.   I. Gilles, Carol.   II. Title.
LB1631.W347   1988   428'.007'12   87–24725
ISBN 0–913461–84–9 (pbk.)

RICHARD C. OWEN PUBLISHERS, INC.
Rockefeller Center
Box 819
New York, New York 10185

PRINTED IN THE UNITED STATES OF AMERICA

Contents

Preface

Whole Language Strategies for Secondary Students is the result of teachers teaching—and learning. The theoretical section, Chapter 1, is the knowledge base that unifies the entire book and lays the foundation for whole language instruction. The term "whole language" has been used by some of us for years, but only recently has it become widely recognized in education. Whole language teachers plan curricula that balance their goals with those of their students. These mutually acceptable goals guide learning experiences. We want to help students develop a taste and appetite for knowledge and ideas, and then to help them satisfy those desires.

At first glance this book may look like another instructional recipe book suggesting a number of activities rather than classroom practices grounded in theory and focused on process. How-to-do-it books present activities for Monday morning, but do not provide a theoretical foundation that will guide the teacher on Tuesday morning. Cookbooks carry the inexperienced cook from one meal to the next. Similarly, instructional cookbooks carry teachers from one activity to the next, but do not empower them with knowledge that leads to flexibility in future decision-making. *Whole Language Strategies for Secondary Students* differs significantly.

Part II consists of strategy lessons that were developed in the context of the use and exploration of language by students and classroom teachers. The value of the strategy lessons rests on the theoretical foundation, and a part of this orientation is briefly restated in the "Why?" section of each strategy lesson.

The strategy lessons have been collected from Mid-Missouri TAWL teachers (Teachers Applying Whole Language) and others. TAWL is a grassroots teacher support organization that takes various names around the world: *Tucsonians Applying Whole Language* (Tucson, Arizona), *Child-Centered Experienced-Based Learning* (Winnepeg, Manitoba, Canada), *Support Maintenance Implementation of Language Expression* (Tempe, Arizona), *The Literacy Connection* (Columbus, Ohio), *Children And Whole Language* (Edmonton, Alberta, Canada), to name a few. A TAWL group (the generic term) can be two teachers talking on the telephone each week about language, learning, students, and curriculum; or it may be a larger group that meets regularly to discuss these issues. Many TAWL groups keep in touch through newletters, and share ideas through workshops, conferences, and books they write. At TAWL meetings teachers share their best ideas as well as their concerns. This collection of strategy lessons represents some of those ideas.

How to Use This Book

In the process of compiling this book we found ourselves in a dilemma: the variety, scope, and number of strategy lessons might lead readers to think this is a "whole language teacher's manual." It is not. Materials can be organized and suggestions outlined, but teachers and students must be involved in decision-making that is influenced by their particular needs, situations, and personalities.

The following is an outline of the contents of the book illustrating its common threads:

After the first theoretical chapter, you are invited into three classrooms (Chapter 2) that exemplify the whole language classrooms where the strategy lessons were born. The similarities among these classrooms can be traced to the theoretical underpinnings of whole language instruction. No two whole language classrooms are alike—this is one of their greatest strengths. The differences are the result of unique individuals—teachers and students—that bring the theory into action.

Chapter 3 contains some of the questions most frequently asked about whole language. The answers come from whole language teachers who continue to raise new questions and refine answers. We have attempted to address some of the major pedagogical and political issues related to whole language instruction, but this ongoing process of inquiry is ultimately up to the individual teacher.

The major portion of the book consists of Part II, the strategy lessons. These are invitations for teachers to make what Ken Goodman calls the "bold decision" to become whole language teachers. This is a personal decision, and this book must be personalized by the teachers and students using it.

Each of Chapters 4–9 is preceded by a discussion of the type and focus of the strategies included. The heart of each strategy lesson is the "Why." The "Who," "How," and "Then What" are suggestions for the audience and procedures for each strategy lesson, and can be modified.

Chapter 10 gives an overview of the place of computers in a whole language classroom.

Certain strategy lessons are an integral and regular part of a whole language curriculum because they are helpful for any language user, whereas others are used selectively, depending on students, materials, and the situation. "Sustained Silent Reading" (see Strategy 4.1), for example, is an activity that is a regular part of the curriculum. Other strategy lessons are more specific, such as those found in the "Extended Literature" section of Chapter 8. Specific strategy lessons are developed for the needs of a particular learner or groups of learners. Some strategies may have been developed for a particular content area, but teachers are encouraged to modify these strategies, to integrate their content area with others.

We can discuss how our classrooms are organized and how strategy lessons are used, but it is the dynamic interplay of the activities, the teacher, and what students learn and do that is meaningful. Each of the strategy lessons could be accompanied by examples of our students' work—a celebration of the successes of the less able as well as those of the stars of the class. There is no room in a whole language classroom for competition. Certainly we expect our students to do the best, *their* personal best. If they happen to fall short we provide the encouragement needed, adjust the classroom atmosphere, or develop new strategy lessons.

As one student said of her whole language special education class: "This is a learning place." We hope that this book contributes something special to your learning place, and that the mutual learning experiences of teachers and students and their desire to learn will never disappear, that students will always be hungry for more. We want our students to extend learning to their out-of-school lives.

Mary Bixby
Shirley R. Crenshaw
Paul Crowley
Carol Gilles
Margaret Henrichs
Donelle Pyle
Frances Reynolds

Columbia, Missouri

Acknowledgments

This book, like the TAWL organization itself, is a collaborative effort. We have shared our time, our best ideas, and , at times, our frustrations. In return we have learned a great deal about language, the writing process, and ourselves.

We wish to thank each strategy contributor. Without your practical and tested strategy lessons this book could not have been written. We also wish to thank Dr. Peter Hasselriis for his suggestions in the initial planning stage; Dr. Patricia Jenkins for her many hours of careful editing and her astute questions; and Dr. Dorothy Watson, who convinced us that this book needed to be written and we were the people to do it. She then gave us the encouragement and support which sustained us in this collaborative effort.

—The Authors

Introduction

It has finally become clear to me why an introduction to a book is the last part written. This last-is-first phenomenon makes sense; the introduction-writer must study the finished manuscript and then draw readers into the text by building a bridge between them and the content. *Whole Language Strategies for Secondary Students* is a case in point. It would have been impossible to write an introduction to this book and then, as some teachers think their students can do with an outline, follow it step-by-step toward writing a finished product. *Strategies* was not created in such a neat and linear way.

In the truest sense of the word this book was written by teachers (many of them), compiled and edited by teachers, tried out by teachers—always with a specific audience in mind: other teachers. Such involvement creates another task for the introduction-writer: Not only must readers be introduced to the text but they need to learn something important about the writers and editors; the readers must know about the beliefs that guided the teachers' work—the same beliefs that continue to guide their work with students and other educators.

The teachers who wrote the strategies in this book believe certain things about students, about language and about how students become proficient writers, readers, listeners, and speakers. The teachers who compiled and edited this book hold those same beliefs, and because of their beliefs made a commitment to bring together teaching/learning experiences that have in positive and authentic ways touched and moved both students and teachers. The editors set out to prepare something of value—something of themselves, something their colleagues deserve, something worthy of students. In doing so they worked closely with teachers, with each other, and, of course, they became intimately familiar with every strategy presented for publication. Activities submitted to them that didn't ring true or failed to be consistent with the new knowledge available about both oral and written language—inauthentic pieces—went into a very large discard pile. No matter how clever or well written the manuscript, it had to be theoretically sound and it had to be applicable to real students in real classrooms.

One characteristic of the writers and editors of this book is that they are persistently straightforward concerning their beliefs about language and teaching; that is, about the theoretical foundation on which they (along with their students) build a literacy program. Because of their resolve to present a rationale, a reason why, it is no surprise that Chapter 1 presents the theory on which they have based and tested the stories and strategies in the book. What teachers facilitate in their classrooms depends on what they understand, believe, and value; therefore, Chapter 1 is presented for the readers' consideration as they form their own beliefs about language learning and teaching.

In Chapter 2 we see students and teachers portrayed in all their reality and humanity on the vivid canvases of three classrooms. In the vignettes we discover implicit descriptions and definitions of terms that the authors and editors of this book use again and again—"meaning centered," "student focused," and "whole language for whole children." We see sensitive, creative, and dedicated teachers making curricular decisions, and orchestrating learning situations after they have looked at their students for ideas and inspiration. We learn from these portrayals that "whole language" means there is no artificial separation of the systems of language and no artificial separation of learning to listen, speak, read, and write. The term "whole student" acknowledges that learners have lives outside the classroom and therefore must have authentic lives within the classroom; that students can be avid and eager language users, learners, resource persons, thinkers, planners, teachers, self-disciplinarians, and friends.

Part II is made up of dozens of carefully prepared invitations that can be accepted in full, in part, or can be rejected outright. This is as it should be, for the authors and editors do not presume that they can hand anyone a preformulated curriculum. These invitations are a professional contribution from a group of teachers who hope that colleagues will consider each offering in light of their students' interests, needs, and personalities. There is also the hope that these strategies may suggest to teachers other invitations that may even more closely touch the lives and language of students.

Dorothy J. Watson

PART I

Theory and Practice

1

Knowing Where We're Coming from:
The Theoretical Bases
by Dorothy J. Watson

■ Introduction

"It ain't enough to know where you're going. You gotta know where you're coming from." The Wiz's advice is just as applicable to teachers attempting to move into new literacy programs as it was to Dorothy when she and Toto were trying to find their way from Oz back to Kansas. If we teachers don't know where we are coming from—that is, if we don't understand the theoretical base that supports our curricula—it is easy to become diverted from our course, wandering aimlessly until we hitch another temporary ride on the next brightly painted bandwagon. Dorothy's yellow brick road is easier to follow—there is less chance of getting lost or weary—if the traveler knows the territory.

The "territory" of *Whole Language Strategies for Secondary Students* has to do with students, their language, and the meaning that is created when students use their language in order to write, read, listen, and speak. That territory is what this chapter is about.

■ Students

Frank Smith (1973) says that in order to help students become proficient language users, teachers need to find out what the students are trying to do—and then help them do it. Yetta Goodman (1978) says that the way we find out what students are trying to do is to become astute observers of them. She calls this enlightened observation *kidwatching*. If we take Smith's and Goodman's advice seriously, it is inevitable that students become the heart of the curriculum. In the words of Jerome Harste (Harste, Woodward, and Burke, 1984) the students become "curricular informants."

In planning for a tenth-grade class no objectives can be written, no assignments made, no plans developed until teachers have a feel for the world of tenth-graders in general, and knowledge of their own tenth-graders in particular. That isn't to say we don't prepare for our students; before meeting them we organize a *possible curriculum* based on all our past experiences with tenth-graders. But only as we meet our students, observe them intelligently, and use them as informants are we able to draw from the potential curriculum appropriate and suitable objectives, assignments, and strategies. Teachers with their students create, change, and are in charge of curriculum.

All the fuss about knowing students, both in general and specifically, comes from the belief that learning occurs when it is personalized and positive, and when it focuses on the strengths and unique abilities of individuals. If we believe that students must be active in the learning process, then we must make sure that they are in situations in which they can contribute. It is very difficult to listen, speak, write, or read about something you know nothing about. When we place students in untenable positions, we can expect disruptive behavior for which, somehow, students get blamed.

We know, but don't always act as if we believe, that students have a life outside the classroom, a life that began its formation years ago without us and includes experiences that might truly surprise us—perhaps even make us gasp. All this diversity of life experiences, both in and out of school, has woven a unique and valuable background of knowledge and information. Ulric Neisser (1976) says that through these personal experiences we form schemata—cognitive structures that help us organize information. As students participate in the school setting, the new information generated there must in some way fit into an existing schema, if knowledge is to flourish and expand.

It isn't enough for students to be active in the learning process; they must also be active in the teaching process. Students in the role of teacher are students who know that they are valued and respected for their strengths, rather than kids who know that they are going to be ignored or hounded because of their "disabilities and disruptions." Compare one student on the same day in two different classrooms: In the first the student spends his time filling in blanks and answering end-of-the-chapter questions—working on someone else's curriculum. It isn't long until the inappropriate work begins to promote inappropriate behavior. In the second classroom the same student is preparing a talk about his father's work, bee-keeping. The student's report will be given to his class and then to a group of elementary students. After careful research the student reads his first draft to a classmate who, while learning a lot about bees, offers good suggestions to the writer. Appropriate work promotes appropriate behavior.

Placing students at the heart of the curriculum isn't to say that teachers have given up or lost control; rather, teachers have moved to a more visionary and creative position—that of coordinator (Webster: "maker of harmonious adjustments") and resource person.

■ Language

Given half a chance, students find language to be fascinating. There are three points to be made from this statement: The first has to do with a definition of language, the second with how any student can come under the spell of language, and the third with invitational teaching.

At the risk of sounding abrupt or trivial, *language* in this book is thought of as a way humans get together; that is, a way they communicate. Further, the arts of communication through language are thought of as writing, reading, speaking, and listening.

By saying "language is fascinating" we mean that *the study* of language, as well as *the use* of language through writing, reading, speaking, and listening, is exciting, satisfying, and captivating—*if* the language user is given half a chance.

In order to give learners the opportunity they deserve—to find writing, reading, speaking, and listening fascinating—teachers need to know not only about their students but about language, about its parts, and about its power as a whole. Then teachers need to know how truly to invite students to come under the spell of language. The strategies in this book are whole language in their makeup and are potential invitations that teachers may want to offer their students. An instructional invitation is similar to a social invitation in that it is an appropriate offer made with grace and with consideration for everyone involved. Like all invitations, there is always the possibility that one will be refused or counter-suggestions given. In a whole language classroom an invitation is never thought of as a stimulus designed to elicit an immediate response or outcome.

Perhaps one of the reasons the less-than-elegant term, whole language, persists as the label for a point of view about language teaching and learning is that the label itself is descriptive. Whole language may mean many things to many people, but its essential meaning is that *all of language in an integrated form must be presented to students* if they are to learn to read and write. Within the complexly organized system of language there are subsystems that work in concert to help humans organize their experiences and mediate meaning. It is these subsystems, the parts of language, that must be kept whole.

Subsystems function naturally and have the power for maximum potential only when they are integrated, not disintegrated. Put another way, when students read they deserve every linguistic sign potential (semantics, grammar, and graphophonemics) available, and every pragmatic sign potential (situational context and prior knowledge) available. Put still another way, real kids deserve real language in real situations.

Let's look at the systems of language that will be kept whole and integrated in the strategies presented in this book.

In Figure 1.1 the pragmatic and linguistic systems of language are represented as concentric circles. The circles are discontinuous to indicate that the systems affect and support each other, and that the culture in which they exist surrounds and permeates all the meaning-giving signs. The culture in which the language and learner thrive affects every aspect of that learner's language. In return, learners as members of societies within a culture help shape their societies, their culture, and their language.

■ Pragmatics

Some may argue that the pragmatic subsystem is not truly linguistic. I want to urge, nevertheless, its consideration as a powerful information-giving subsystem within the language arts. Pragmatics is language in use and has to do with the reader's prior knowledge and with how language has meaning within the situational context in which it is used.

Prior knowledge has to do with information gained in other times and other places, knowledge that students potentially can bring to their reading and writing, listening, and speaking both in and out of school.

Situational context involves authors' and speakers' intentions and readers' and listeners' expectations—all that has to do with the *why* of literacy. Just

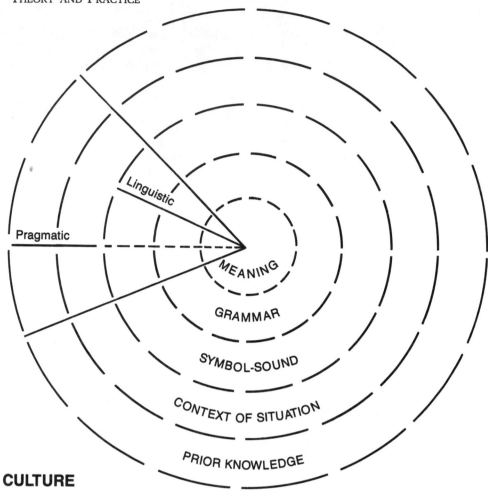

CULTURE

FIGURE 1.1 Pragmatic and Linguistic Systems of Language (Watson, Burke, and Goodman, 1983)

as importantly, situational context involves the circumstances of the event—*where, when, and how* the reading or writing is taking place. For example, when we direct our attention to street signs we *expect* to get information about how and where we should drive; and when we open our science books we *expect* certain words, writing styles, and formats that will help us mediate meaning. If we are lucky the writer of the street sign and the author of the science books have *intentions* that are consistent with our *expectations*. If we are not so lucky we may find ourselves going the wrong way in both traffic and science.

■ **Semantics**

Semantics has to do with the reader's, writer's, listener's, and speaker's sense of meaning. This subsystem emerges naturally from and along with the pragmatic system and is powerfully influenced by the culture. When one is reading and writing it can be said that meaning is not on the paper, not in the black marks and white spaces found or placed on the page, but rather in the heads of the reader and the author—those who are actively choosing words to create meaning. The purpose of activating language is to mediate meaning for those who are using it. If we had no meaning there would be no need for grammar or for the surface features of print and sound. Semantics (meaning) is therefore the linguistic subsystem that makes the other systems necessary.

Teachers in whole language programs are deeply concerned with the way meanings are represented by words and the relationship of words and meanings with other words and meanings. They are keenly aware that meanings are not always represented in the same way by students, textbook writers, editors, and teachers. The student's meaning and the language chosen to represent that meaning are at the heart of whole language programs.

■ Grammar

The grammatical subsystem provides a predictable framework that supports meaning. Without such a framework we could only guess at an author's intentions. For example, if we were to read the words: *paint, green, I'm, to, house, going, the,* we would likely be confused. But if we arranged the words in a grammatically acceptable string (used syntax) we might read: "I'm going to paint the house green." If we chose a different syntactical arrangement we might read: "I'm going to paint the green house." If we selected a slightly different inflection we would read: "I'm going to paint the greenhouse." Three different messages and our knowledge of grammar, along with the pragmatic situation, help us make sense of them.

Besides syntax itself, function words and word endings provide grammatical information. Function words (such as articles, verb auxiliaries, prepositions, and conjunctions) keep content words together. They signal the relationship between and among words when they are in the context of a complete utterance that has meaning. To give students isolated words, as in a vocabulary drill, is to remove grammatical information. When this is done, the words are removed not only from the on-the-page contextuality of any discourse but also from the off-the-page contextuality of any pragmatic setting.

■ Graphophonemics

The symbol-sound, or graphophonemic subsystem, has two subsets: the visual information of language, which includes graphemes (letters), punctuation marks, capital and lower-case forms, italics, white spaces, underlining, etc.; and the phonemic, or sound system, of the language. No one denies that we need the symbols provided by the graphemic system. If we had no print we would have little or nothing to read, unless a Braille or hand-signing form were used. Symbol-sound information should be used in concert with the other subsystems of language in order to *confirm* predictions made by the listener or reader. Problems arise when there is an instructional preoccupation with the graphophonemic subsystem—such as sounding out letters, syllables, words— and in teaching the rules for doing so.

A whole language literacy program is one in which all the linguistic and pragmatic systems are kept whole so that they can support each other and in doing so support the language user. When the language systems are separated for study, as sometimes happens during formal instruction that has a narrow focus, meaning is the first subsystem to be destroyed. And when there is no meaning there is no need for language.

■ Creating Meaning by Reading

Reading is a process in which the reader and the text come together for the purpose of creating meaning. Authors use their linguistic and pragmatic knowledge in order to write the text. Readers bring their linguistic and pragmatic knowledge to the text in order to construct meaning. After listening to hundreds of students read and then analyzing their miscues (deviations from the text), Kenneth Goodman (1982) concluded that the strategies needed to process text—that is, to read—are: sampling from the text, predicting at all linguistic levels, confirming the predictions or rejecting the predictions and predicting again, correcting, and in the process integrating on-the-page information with off-the-page information (see Figure 1.2).

Teachers in whole language programs are aware that, given the same text, readers do not necessarily construct the same meanings. This individuality is recognized, respected, and utilized in the literacy program. With this understanding, whole language teachers are careful not to label readers as low, average, high. They realize that all of us are more proficient when reading something of interest than when we are superficially involved in discourse that reaps no benefits or joy. Students know, too, that text can be "inconsiderate" if it is written without regard for the readers' interests and needs, or if its style is lifeless and its organizing structure is nonsupportive of the reader.

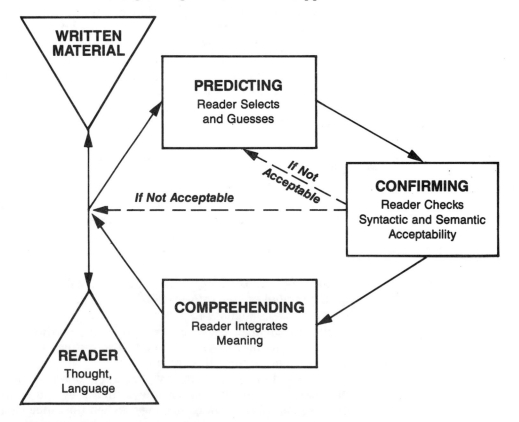

FIGURE 1.2 Models of Reading (Y. Goodman and Burke, 1980)

The purpose of reading instruction is not to stamp out readers' miscues; rather, the purpose is to help students control the reading strategies of sampling, predicting, confirming, and integrating meaning. When students and teachers move from an "uptight model" of reading (Goodman, 1982) an interesting thing happens: Readers gain control of the process; their miscues get better (e.g., they make good substitutions); and the number of miscues diminishes as well.

■ Creating Meaning by Writing

There is a growing concern in this country over the declining proficiency in writing. The back-to-the-basics answer to this concern focuses students' attention on spelling, grammar, vocabulary, and even handwriting as discrete, isolated skills. The research of Donald Graves (1978) and others strongly suggests that writing should be thought of as a process rather than a product, and that to control the process we must "let them write." Students are invited daily to write by drawing on their own experiences and generating their own topics.

The writing process begins, as does the reading process, with meaning. Also, just as reading starts before the book is open, writing starts before the pencil touches the page. Pre-writing, or rehearsing, may include talking over ideas with friends, getting more information, making a list or chart, sketching, or quietly mulling over ideas. Rehearsing allows the writer freedom to tap background experience and to experiment with, but not be committed to, a specific topic or theme. Rehearsing enables writers to find their topics and their voices; thus eliminating the response, "I don't know what to write about," to the invitation to write.

Writers create through a series of drafts in which they revise by rethinking personal meanings and by reorganizing ideas. To help in drafting, effective writing programs involve a variety of writing conferences. Teachers and students learn to ask questions of writers that will support their writing but not interfere with text ownership. Editing takes place after drafting. Here, teachers or peers may help the writer conventionalize spelling, punctuation, and grammar. A premature concern for correctness of form during the composing and revising phases may inhibit thoughtful and creative writing. In truth, the desire to write may vanish if students are taught to view correctness as more important than meanings and messages. In a classroom in which writing serves a variety of purposes, some writing such as journals, personal responses, and written conversations need never be revised or edited; editing depends on the pragmatic context.

Students in control of their own writing decide which pieces are to be edited for "publication." A publication or celebration of a piece can involve actually sending it to the school newspaper or to a magazine for young people. Less formal, but just as satisfying, celebrations can involve making a book in which a short biography of the author is given, or by highlighting the piece during an author's circle, or by pinning it on a special bulletin board.

■ Invitations to Meaning Construction

We probably can all read or write at the command of someone else. But even if we like the person who issues the command, we won't like the command.

Sometimes students "luck out:" The teacher commands them to read or write, and they reluctantly do so only to discover that the story they are told to read is gripping, or that all nine muses have inspired them to great writing. It doesn't happen often. Yet teachers who know students, know language, know literature, and know how to issue an invitation are sure to have writers, readers, speakers, and listeners in their classes.

Modeling has a large part to play in issuing a good invitation. When teachers themselves are reading and writing; when they enter into a discussion without taking over; when they become learners as well as teachers; they are demonstrating proficient and effective language behavior. Demonstrating with an invitation says: "This is the way I do it, but you know different things about this subject, so you will do it differently."

When teachers first move from mandates to invitations it often takes a while for students to understand that invitations can be modified or even refused if credible alternatives can be presented. If an alternative or counter-invitation is presented, the teacher and student need to discuss its merits and make decisions together about the curriculum. Just as some invitations are unacceptable, some alternatives are unacceptable. If this is the case both students and teachers need to know the reasons.

Students in a whole language classroom will offer literacy invitations to each other as well as to the teacher. When this happens, it is obvious that the program has vitality; it is one in which all participants are real users of language.

2

Theory in Use
Reading, Writing, and Learning: Three Classroom Vignettes

Chapter 2 gives the reader a glimpse of three very different classrooms. The first is an American Studies and English block class at the eighth-grade level; the second is a sophomore biology class; and the third is a special education class. These vignettes were selected because they are diverse but representative of how learning takes place in whole language classrooms. The teachers in each classroom hold similar theoretical beliefs. They share attitudes toward students and themselves as learners. In all three classrooms the teachers are innovative and willing to risk making changes to challenge the students and enhance learning. Bob Steffes and Greg Grupe feel strongly about the necessity of reading and writing in the curriculum; they have joined forces to emphasize language across the curriculum in their American Studies and English block. Ilayna Pickett, the high-school biology teacher, is willing to risk reading *The Lorax* (a read-aloud children's book) to her classes, because she knows *that* particular book will help her students to question, to investigate, and to challenge environmental issues. In these two vignettes the focus is broad. We see whole language from a teacher's point of view in a very large class of fifty students (in American Studies/English) and in a science class of thirty students. In the story of John in the special education class the focus shifts to one student labeled "learning disabled." The in-depth study takes place over a period of three years, which allows us to see how whole language teaching works over time from a student's perspective.

In all three classrooms the subject matter may be diverse, but the environment, the roles of the participants, and the role that language plays are similar. Instructional strategy lessons are crucial components in a whole language classroom. A strategy lesson is an instructional procedure in which all the appropriate language cueing systems (the meaning system, the grammatic system, the sound-symbol system, and the context in which the language event occurs) are used in order to strengthen readers' abilities to process written language, that is, to sample, predict, confirm, and construct meaning (Goodman, 1982). Strategy lessons are written to meet specific needs, and they can be written for use by one student, a small group of students, or an entire class. The lessons, which incorporate reading, writing, speaking, listening, and thinking, are practical applications of theory. Specific strategy lessons are discussed in the second part of this book. However, the vignettes demonstrate how strategy lessons can be incorporated into an entire curriculum.

■ Language Across the Curriculum: American Studies and English Block Class Experience

"Hey, you got your newspaper story done?" Maverick asks another junior high student as they enter the room. "You know I'm typing all the stories, and we got a deadline to meet. I think we should name our paper *Southern Comfort!*"

Maverick and his group of five students gather in one corner as others enter the room, which quickly fills with fifty students and comes alive with their questions.

"Do you have the illustrations done?"

"How many slaves did Harriet Tubman free?"

"What if I'm supposed to be for the South, but I really don't believe in slavery? Can I be for the South and be against slavery?"

Greg Grupe and Bob Steffes enter, and the students settle down.

"Now you all know that today is a workday," Grupe begins. "You need to meet in your groups and continue working on the newspaper. You have chosen to be from the North or the South. Please remember that your news stories, features, advertisements, editorials, and obituaries must be from the Civil War period. If you don't recall what was popular at that time, look around the room." He points to the assortment of books, pictures, and photographs on the side cabinets. "You will be revising with a friend and then selecting an editor from your group. Mr. Steffes and I will circulate to help you and answer questions."

Steffes, an English teacher, and Grupe, an American Studies teacher, have initiated an exciting program at Jefferson Junior High School in Columbia, Missouri. They teach a daily two-hour block course in a room large enough to accommodate a double class. The focus of the course is learning about American Studies and English through intensive reading and writing. The Civil War unit, lasting three weeks, is one of many completed throughout the year. Other units include Native Americans, the Revolutionary War, American Inventors, and World Wars I and II. Although the cooperation is mainly between American Studies and English, the Reading Department also shares in some units (such as the Revolutionary War) by encouraging students to read historical biographies from the period being studied.

When students study the "Brothers' War" they examine the causes of the Civil War, the events and personalities of that period, and the results of the struggle to reunite the nation. At the same time students become more powerful writers, as they learn about and practice various kinds of writing. They compare and contrast Jefferson Davis and Ulysses S. Grant. They read about and characterize Abraham Lincoln, Harriet Tubman, and Robert E. Lee. Grupe and Steffes use instructional strategy lessons (many of which are found in this book) to help students extend their abilities and learn content. Students are encouraged to use writing to discover what they know and to make connections between concepts. The writing is not always lengthy. A ten-minute writing period to detail the strengths and weaknesses of the North and South, or perhaps write reactions to a short story based on historical fact, helps the student both to understand the concept and to practice composing. Longer compositions, such as rewriting the "Gettysburg Address" in modern English or constructing a newspaper from the Civil War period (see Strategy 7.4), provide ample opportunities for revising and editing.

Resources for such activities are extensive. Volumes of books about the Civil War era, including books actually written during that time and books about Missouri during the Civil War, line the walls. Films like *The Autobiography of Miss Jane Pittman* help bring the realities of the Reconstruction Era to students. In other units, such as the Depression, personal accounts from the community offer students a chance to practice interviewing, while learning history from a first-hand narrative. Also, during several of the units, students have the option of selecting factual books or historical fiction to extend their learning.

At the end of each unit a magazine of written work is published by students. A group of students cull through all writings, revise in groups, and meet after school to enter some writings on the word processor. Copies are made and each student receives a copy of the magazine—a summary of the highlights of the unit, including literature and art. All students are "published" at least once during the year. (For more information see Strategy 7.9.)

Assessment also encourages reading and writing. Many tests are essay or an essay-objective combination, where students apply the types of writing they have been practicing. Besides testing as evaluation, students have opportunities to evaluate themselves (their writings, attitudes, and work habits), members of their group (through peer revision and peer editing), and their teachers. Grupe and Steffes welcome input from students and other teachers to consistently improve the units.

In this class students are asked to help make curricular decisions and to help one another learn. Students are given options for meeting various educational objectives. For example, one of the objectives in the Civil War unit is to have students realize the effects of the war on daily life. To meet that objective students read specified pages in a text, listen to class lectures and discussions, and then choose one of the following options:

1. Write a series of letters from a Northern cousin to a Southern cousin in which you describe what life is like at home during the war. What are your biggest fears and your biggest problems? Are there shortages? What is different about your life now from before the war?
2. Assume the role of a white Southerner during the war. Write at least three diary entries in which you describe how your life is different now and what problems you face that never occurred to you before the war.
3. Assume the role of a black slave during the war who is keeping an illegal diary. What problems are you having? How is your owner treating you? What will your life be like after the war?

For many activities students are encouraged to write with a partner, review one another's work, collaborate in dramatizing historic events, or discuss in groups. As Grupe puts it: "You all add to each other's knowledge. We're all resources in here."

How do students like this approach? Steffes' and Grupe's humor is the first element that students identify. But they soon realize the class is both entertaining *and* challenging. They enjoy the fast pace and the original activities designed to pique curiosity, hone concepts, and provide various types of appropriate practice. There is no bleary-eyed drowsing in this class. Students are challenged to live and breathe history, to give their best, to work harder than ever before, to produce. In return, students receive the best of Steffes and Grupe, who are very positive with them. They watch students excelling and spread the word to other teachers.

Although the program has received the admiration of both staff and administration, students have the final voice. Recently the student council rated the teachers at JJHS and presented the results at a faculty meeting. Of Bob Steffes and Greg Grupe they said: "Unique teaching methods . . . They make learning a whole new experience . . . They treat students as adults." Such accolades are rare from junior high students. On the last day of school Grupe asked his students: "How many of you had trouble writing when you came in here last fall?" Every hand shot up. "Now put down your hand if writing has gotten easier." The hands fell. For Steffes and Grupe the year was a success.

■ Whole Language in the Biology Lab

Every available inch of wall space in this basement biology classroom seems to have something on it to look at, read, and ponder. There are colorful posters of the body's systems; plants in various places; fish tanks; and a red, white, and blue skeleton (red and blue show where muscles are attached) standing sentinel-like at the front of the room. Stacks of magazines such as *Smithsonian, Audubon, Scientific American, Science Digest, National Geographic,* and *National Wildlife* line one counter and on nearby shelves are teacher Ilayna Pickett's personal collection of books. Titles such as *Sand County Almanac, Lives of a Cell, The Panda's Thumb, Silent Spring, The Medusa and the Snail,* and *The Curious Naturalist* reflect this teacher's love of science, language, and books.

Ilayna Pickett, biology teacher, presides with humor and exuberance over the Rock Bridge High School biology lab. The tenth-grade biology curriculum emphasizes first the person and the body's systems and then turns to the person and the environment. Audio-visual materials, print, graphics, and lab experiments help present concepts. The textbook is secondary and used as a resource, for Pickett believes in a multi-text approach. To clarify and extend the concepts taught, lab notebooks and learning logs are kept, along with writing assignments. Discussions and quiz reviews are lively and are punctuated with quips and jokes which elicit answers and comments from even the most reticent students. Tests are usually a combination of essay and objective items. This feels like a real learning environment; it is a science classroom alive with language.

A good illustration of how Pickett incorporates language (reading, writing, listening, speaking, and thinking) in the tenth-grade biology units is to follow her and her students through one of the segments in the unit on ecology. This particular sequence is based on reading *The Lorax* by Dr. Seuss (yes—a read-aloud children's book in high school). *The Lorax* is the story of the greedy Once-ler who chopped down all the Truffula Trees to make Threeds (a garment of sorts). The Lorax, who spoke for the trees, warned of dire consequences, but was paid no heed; and then, sure enough, the balance of nature was tipped and dreadful things happened in the environment.

This segment with *The Lorax* is used to introduce the unit on ecology. The objectives of the unit are that students become aware of factors contributing to environmental problems, form their own viewpoints on these factors, and express themselves by supporting or refuting an environmental issue. It is a powerful, engrossing beginning to the study of people and the impact of their interaction with the environment. Some of the later segments deal with pollution, population, ecosystems, and ethics.

The segment begins with a brainstorming session about the word "unless," which is the message the Lorax leaves behind. The students write what they think the word means, and discuss their ideas before Pickett reads the story aloud. Later they write their impressions of the story, and share those within small groups. Next, they divide into groups representing different people or characters from the story, such as the Once-ler, a member of the Once-ler family, a consumer wanting to buy a Threed, a consumer who does not want a Threed, an environmentalist, a sportsman, a high-school student, and the Lorax. As they pretend to be these characters they brainstorm how the situation in their town came about, how they feel about it, and what should be done. Next students are asked to write an editorial that would appear in the town newspaper presenting their concerns and ideas. Editorials are published (printed in some way; i.e., put on ditto, mimeo, or just posted on the bulletin board) so all groups can read and discuss them. Groups are asked to brainstorm real-life problems that parallel the story, then categorize the problems and rank them, thus identifying the five most pressing concerns. At this point there is a class discussion and reading of current periodicals that relate to the identified problems.

The next step in the activity is library research. Students choose an environmental issue they are most interested in, research methods and sources are identified, and several days are spent in the library. Notes are taken on the library reading. Instead of writing a report, students write a letter to a person (e.g., Congressperson or a company president) having authority or impact on an issue. The entire writing process is used to compose this letter (from rough draft to revising to editing to final copy ready for mailing). The letters are mailed, and when the replies arrive they are shared and discussed by the entire class.

As demonstrated by this example, writing, reading, speaking, and listening are incorporated naturally into all the units. Writing to learn, to clarify, to deepen comprehension is used throughout the units in biology. Reading to learn and to extend concepts from a variety of materials and sources is standard practice. Above all, independent thinking is encouraged through generating, testing, and confirming hypotheses; expressing and defending opinions; and integrating new information into the daily lives of students.

■ John

As a seventh-grader John was enrolled in the typical junior high school curriculum, with one exception: He was not in an English class but rather in a special education class for students labeled "learning disabled." This label was not new to John. He had been singled out early in his educational career, particularly for his lack of success in writing and reading. Descriptions such as "perceptual motor difficulties" and "processing deficit" were used to describe John's school problems.

Like most junior high school students John did not want to be thought of as different. From the first day he made this clear to his L.D. teacher. John frequently said that he didn't need the class. He came in late each day so that no one would see him enter "that room." He made sure that the door was closed for the duration of his stay, and he skipped out quickly when the bell rang.

John's teacher hated the label as much as John did, but for different reasons. As a whole language teacher he was comfortable concentrating on students' linguistic strengths, not their difficulties. Instead of lumping kids into ill-defined categories he accepted the abilities of individual language users as a starting point. Instead of describing the class of four boys as "learning disabled" the teacher gave them the name "unlabeled gifted."

John was not prepared for what happened each day in this class. He was used to instruction that reflected the traditional special education paradigm: After a "specific learning disability" has been diagnosed, remediation is prescribed—just like in the hospital. But in this class, instead of getting workbook drills on specific reading skills, John was given whole texts. Instead of fine motor exercises, he was given a pen and paper. John didn't know what to do.

"This is boring" was a common complaint about daily journal writing. "Why do we have to read?" the group asked about Sustained Silent Reading. Rather than preaching about the virtues of reading and writing, John's teacher promoted these activities by engaging in them himself. He helped students find books and poems that they could not resist. When students said they hated poetry, Shel Silverstein's poems proved them wrong. Books by S.E. Hinton were read aloud; and students were riveted by the stories. The teacher did not tell students to read and write because "he said so"; rather, he made it clear that this classroom was a place for reading and writing, and if the students did not enjoy these activities it was because they had not found the right book or they had not written something that was important to them. He let them know that he would help them discover these pleasures of reading and writing—by reading and writing. Students were helped to see their experiences as rich and worthy of the written word. The shelves were stocked with a wide variety of books appealing to different interests and abilities. John's experiences with literacy included "switching roles" with the teacher by sharing his knowledge of World War II (see Strategy 4.18), interacting with classmates through written conversations (see Strategy 4.4), and participating in reading conferences (see Strategy 9.5). Reading, writing, speaking, and listening were the curriculum whether John was studying fighter planes, working on a social studies assignment, reading about motorcycles, or learning about the circulatory system.

John was a good student. Even though he disliked many of the class activities, he participated. Reading was not difficult for him; he could read all of his textbooks and he occasionally read books or magazines about war machinery for enjoyment. But John hated to write; his stories and journal entries were rarely more than three or four lines long and they lacked "individuality." Here was a student with a lot to say, but written language was not his medium of choice. Encouragement from the teacher took the form of lengthy written responses in John's journal, identifying topics John brought up as interesting ideas for stories, and typing chosen finished products to share with others.

Much of John's insecurity about his writing came from its unconventionality. He frequently left off word endings or omitted words, and his spelling did not always reflect sound-symbol relationships. His teacher began to wonder if John would ever gain control of these conventions.

As the year progressed, the tension about literacy and learning was eased through a program that focused on students' interests and strengths. Success and progress went hand in hand. John was immersed in language and began to take part in classroom activities willingly. By the end of the year he decided that this wasn't such a bad class after all and that he wouldn't mind being in it next year.

The following year John chose the unlabeled gifted program over English because he felt English would be too difficult. He sat at a table each day, wrote in his journal, and then picked up what he needed to work on, continuing projects or beginning new ones. For over a year he had been given choices and thus had learned how to deal with them. John engaged in conversation about his current interests in and out of school. Rather than viewing this as "off-task behavior" the teacher recognized the importance of the various social purposes oral and written language serve and the need to offer opportunities for varied language use. The eighth-grade classroom was a workshop in which both students and teacher learned.

John was lucky to be in a school in which many teachers incorporated writing in their curricula. John made the decision to become a writer. He knew he had good ideas and he knew that conveying meaning was the important part of writing. He wrote about an imaginary trip through Europe for his geography class. Taking on the role of a Yankee in the American Studies class, John wrote letters home from the front describing his experiences. His unlabeled gifted teacher had become a facilitator. As John finished a draft he would bring it to his teacher and ask him to "fix the spelling and punctuation." After a brief conference about content John was satisfied that he had said all he wanted to say in his piece. John was making decisions about his own writing, and his teacher respected the author's ownership of the piece. John needed to take control. The teacher gladly became John's secretary and "fixed the spelling and punctuation."

As John's production increased, so did his confidence and ability. The natural questions and comments by the teacher and fellow students helped John look at his writing from his audience's perspective; and he began to make more substantive content revisions. His teacher continued to make the final editorial revisions.

One day, when John brought a piece for editing, the teacher did not pick up his pen. Rather, he said, "John, you know where periods go and that sentences start with capital letters. And you know how to spell some words. Why don't you make the changes you can make. If you think a word is spelled in a non-standard form, circle it and try it another way. If you have no idea how else it could be spelled, just circle it." Rather than telling John to go outside himself to a dictionary for spelling help, John's teacher wanted to impress upon him that he already knew a lot about spelling if he would take the time to discover it. This was the first time John had considered such a notion. Immediately John saw that he had control of conventions as well as the expression of his ideas. The omitted words were inserted; the continuous text was punctuated; and the spelling that had looked so unconventional became quite logical and, more often than not, standard. John now had the confidence to take an English class in ninth grade, but he also wanted to remain in the unlabeled gifted class because he "learned a lot in there."

As a ninth-grader John continued using this class as a workshop to pursue varied, new literary and learning ventures. He discovered an adventure series (over sixty books) packed with action. Although these books lacked merit by some literary standards, they were John's literature. He read two to five of these books a week, enjoying them immensely, sometimes to the neglect of his schoolwork. John read assigned novels and short stories for his English class, but the adventure novels were what he chose to read. His unlabeled gifted teacher respected his choices, while encouraging him to expand his interests.

John decided that he would choose a book out of the classroom library. He picked *The Plague* by Albert Camus. This was quite a change from his usual reading, and caused him enough difficulty that he returned to his adventure novels. One day John asked his teacher about *1984* by George Orwell. During the year 1984 much press coverage had been given to Orwell's book, and John had heard about it. Student and teacher talked about the book and John decided that he wanted to read it. Rather than writing a book report John kept a response log in which he raised questions, pondered ambiguous ideas, made interpretations, and stated his feelings and attitudes. It was his usual procedure to read until he came to a logical stopping point, then to write for five to ten minutes in his log (see Strategy 6.1 for more on learning logs). It was obvious from his discussions and his log entries that John loved *1984*.

At the same time John was reading *1984* in his unlabeled gifted class, he was reading *Romeo and Juliet* in the English class. John turned to his teacher in the middle of writing in his response log and said, "You know, *1984* is a lot like *Romeo and Juliet*." "How's that?" his teacher asked. "Well, in both stories two people are trying to love each other while outside forces are trying to keep them apart for their own political reasons." After John's teacher regained his composure he let John know that not only was this observation extremely insightful but that it was the first time that he had ever considered the connection.

Learning disabled? On the last day of ninth grade John gave his teacher a beautifully written expository essay discussing the themes that John gleaned from *1984*. He thought his teacher "might like it."

Postscript

Could John have gotten where he did without the teacher and the interaction in this classroom? Probably not. John had a great deal of ability and potential, as all learners do. Through consistency and encouragement (as opposed to "that didn't work, let's try something else") John's teacher facilitated his development. Because he knows about language, learning, and kids, John's teacher helped John make some important changes in his attitudes and strategies.

Moving on to high school, John decided that he did not need to be in a learning disabilities class. His teacher agreed. John has had some difficulty in higher level math, but not in his English classes. Today, John writes essays and reads a variety of novels on his own. Recently he was discussing books with his former teacher and said that he had just bought a book he wanted to read—*The Plague*.

John has not decided where he wants to go to college, but he is sure that he wants to go to the University of Michigan for his master's degree.

■ How Are These Three Classrooms Alike?

What do a combined English-social studies class, a biology class, and a special education class have in common? The content is diverse, yet in all three classes learners are active participants and reading and writing are used extensively to enhance learning. They are all whole language classrooms with common features that reflect the teachers' notions about students' language and the learning process. These commonalities involve the environment, the roles of participants, and the role of language (reading, writing, speaking, and listening) in the curriculum.

These classrooms are "littered with literacy" (Harste, 1984). The posters and papers on the walls reflect the interests of students and teachers. Student-made maps, charts, diagrams, stories, poems, essays, and artwork line the walls. Multiple textbooks, trade books from various libraries, and the teachers' favorite books fill the shelves. Films, videos, charts, maps, and student-authored pieces are used to extend learning.

Environment is more than room arrangement and book selection. In these classrooms there is a feeling of warmth and acceptance. Students and teachers regard themselves as learners, and all are valued in the learning process. Students are encouraged to use each other and the teachers as resources. Learning is a team effort, or, as Grupe puts it: "We're all resources in here." Students help one another—to brainstorm new ideas, to revise pieces, to edit written work, to read in pairs, and to discuss their reading in groups.

The teacher plays an important role in a whole language classroom. Harste and Burke (1977, p. 32) found that ". . . despite atheoretical statements, teachers are theoretical and despite lack of knowledge about reading theory, per se, students are theoretical in the way in which they approach learning to read." Teachers work from their belief systems about children, language, and learning. These beliefs are reflected in their classrooms, guiding the curriculum and the kinds of instructional decisions made. Let's consider some of the beliefs that are reflected in the three classrooms.

All three are alive with reading and writing. The teachers believe that students learn to read by reading and to write by writing (Smith, 1979). Students are given opportunities to read authentic language in the form of books, magazines, newspapers, and so on. These teachers believe that students must be given real texts of reasonable length to help them get a footing and grab onto meaning. Language is not simplified and contrived. There is no attempt to encourage students to rely on "high-interest, low-vocabulary" books, which purportedly try to simplify the reading process by using shorter words and shortening sentence length. Attempts to simplify texts often actually make them more difficult to read because the structures and word choices used in an effort to make the sentences shorter are unnatural, unfamiliar, and nonsensical. Rather than relying on simplified texts, these teachers strive to build the students' backgrounds, through films, discussions, "hands-on" experiences, and alternative reading. The textbook then serves as a summary, not an introduction to new ideas.

In the three settings the teachers see themselves as facilitators or organizers. They enjoy learning from fellow teachers and students. Setting up a classroom in which students have opportunities to explore interests, make decisions, and become responsible for their own learning takes a great deal of organization and collaboration on the part of the teacher and the students. Discipline is handled firmly, but with humor. Ms. Pickett, the high-school biology teacher, challenges her students to investigate issues for themselves. Grupe's style is quick and full of witticisms. Students have to pay attention to see if they are part of his jokes on a given day. John's teacher encourages him to make decisions regarding his own learning, and then to act on these decisions. Many special education students are instruction-bound; that is, they attempt to do exactly what the teacher asks, nothing more and nothing less. When they are confronted with a teacher who is a facilitator, they are eased into the decision-making process. With humor and guidance they find they can make their own decisions and take control of their own learning.

Although reading and writing are highlighted in these classrooms, the main focus is the content—American Studies, English, or science. Reading and writing are vehicles used to enhance content learning. The teachers encourage students to get involved with the content, to delve deeply and become "experts" in some area. Students are given opportunities to do research on specific interests and to present that information to the rest of the class. All of the students' knowledge is broadened, and the individual student or group of students is allowed to move beyond the survey level.

In these classes the teachers believe that effective learning occurs when unfamiliar concepts are related to personal knowledge. Events are contextualized in various ways, so students can relate new concepts to something they already know. Grupe and Steffes ask students to make decisions as if they were in the historical period being studied: What would they have done if they were slaves or plantation owners in the Civil War? What would they have brought aboard the Mayflower? How would they have felt as a sixteen-year-old soldier fighting Hitler in World War II? These kinds of activities challenge students to feel the culture of the period. History becomes real—actual situations and people, not just facts. Ms. Pickett challenges her students to social action. When they look at the hazards of pollution they are encouraged to solve real community problems and to relay their solutions to their congressperson or city representative. The science concepts they study are related directly to their community and their lives. These kinds of activities move the curriculum from the school to the community and beyond.

Special education students visit college teacher-preparation classes to tell these students what it is like to be in a "special class." They practice their literacy talents and present poems, stories, and art-work to show prospective teachers that when students are challenged to do their best and to work through their strengths, they can be successful.

When concepts are personalized and the curriculum moves beyond the classroom, students' world views expand. They begin to take more responsibility, both for their own learning and in their own community. Steffes and Grupe have eighth-grade students who take the responsibility of coming in after school to publish an historical magazine. Special education students have taken it upon themselves to help teach younger students at a "Parent and Reading Fair" each year. They spend an evening reading and writing with young children, so that parents can attend sessions to learn more about literacy.

The teachers use all the resources available—their knowledge about students, language, and learning—to create classrooms where learning is exciting and everyone is able to contribute. Strategy lessons are designed by teachers to help students develop their reading, writing, speaking, and listening abilities as they learn content material. The strategy lessons may be designed for one student, as in the case of John, or for an entire class of students.

As teachers use the strategies they become better "kidwatchers," or enlightened observers (Y. Goodman, 1978). They watch students to see where they are having successes and difficulties. This information leads to individual conferences, quick "mini-lessons" for a small group of students, or possibly to another strategy lesson. Thus, ongoing evaluation is built into the notion of using strategy lessons. Teachers depend on their strong theoretical base, their uses of appropriate strategy lessons, and their respect for students to become decision-makers in the learning process that will enable their students to write better, to read better, and to reason better (Harste, 1985). This collaborative effort ensures that students have successful learning experiences.

3

Questions and Answers about a Whole Language Curriculum

Whole language teaching involves reflecting on theory and practice in light of what students do. Questions relating to curriculum, evaluation, language, learning, and politics are never exhausted. Whole language teachers must continually address important issues related to instruction because they are responsible for developing curriculum.

This chapter addresses frequently asked questions concerning whole language. The questions and answers, though, continue to change and evolve as practice informs theory and theory informs practice.

■ Is There Uniformity in a Whole Language Program?

If I were to visit several whole language classrooms, would I see similar things? Whole language teaching is not a hodge-podge of "fun" activities. Activities and materials will differ just as students and classes differ. Dorothy Watson (1986) identifies the components of a whole language program that are integrated into the curriculum in some manner daily. These components are:

1. Students are read to or told stories every day; they need to be involved with language.
2. Students have time to read and write independently every day; they need to practice oral and written language.
3. The world of the student is brought into the classroom every day; this helps students to make connections between their outside lives and school and to know that they are valued.
4. Reading and writing are brought to conscious awareness every day; this helps students to develop and enhance effective strategies for reading and writing.

■ How Do Strategy Lessons and Activities Relate to Purposes of Language Use?

The purpose of using language is communication. A whole language classroom operates on the belief that people learn language and learn about language by using it in natural contexts. Such activities as Sustained Silent Reading, reading to find information for projects, teachers' reading and telling stories to students, and students' writing to each other are social, communicative occasions in which reading, writing, speaking, and listening can be strengthened. The strategy lessons in this book create occasions to use language for the purpose of communication.

■ What Are the Differences between a Strategy and a Strategy Lesson?

Language use involves the orchestration of complex cognitive and social processes, and language users must make decisions on a number of levels as they read, write, speak, and listen. In reading, for instance, the reader must decide what to do when something unfamiliar is encountered. The array of options the reader has at that point are called strategies, the intuitive choices that learners make to help them construct meaning. Possible strategies include "sounding out" a word, looking it up in the dictionary, asking someone, or skipping the unfamiliar and reading on to get additional information. These strategies are modified and personalized by each learner.

Strategy lessons are opportunities for learners to practice using their strategies in meaningful experiences. These lessons create contexts to help the language user make good choices to construct meaning in written and oral language. Strategy lessons grow out of the needs of individual learners, are meant to be modified, and should be used with relevant materials. Extended literature activities, for example, offer readers specific opportunities to use reading strategies in the context of literature exploration.

Strategy lessons grow out of the strategies that students employ. The strategy lessons in this book are grouped by the types of materials that they require and by the types of strategies they encourage students to utilize. These lessons are part of a total program, and decisions about their use and adaptation come alive in the hands of teachers and students.

■ How Do I Know if My Students Are Effective Readers?

Effective readers use their backgrounds, experiences, and knowledge of the world and of language to construct meaning from print. They are linguistic risk-takers, and have a vast repertoire of reading strategies from which they select, depending on their purposes and the type of text (connected discourse) they are reading. They use their own wealth of information, as well as print information, in order to make predictions, confirm their predictions, and integrate what they comprehend from the text.

Effective readers read for a variety of purposes, approaching unfamiliar material with confidence that it will make sense and that they can construct meaning. Readers may read to remember and/or read to understand. Effective readers read to understand, and in doing so they also read to remember.

Effective reading is making meaning, not an exact duplication of the text.

All readers miscue—that is, deviate from the expected response—for a variety of reasons. Effective readers make miscues that are grammatically and syntactically acceptable; their miscues are meaningful and move them through the text. Effective readers are more likely to enjoy reading because their focus is on making sense.

■ What Is the Teacher's Role in a Whole Language Classroom?

The teacher plays many roles. The teacher is an astute observer who watches and listens to students to find out each one's abilities, unique experiences, interests, and needs. The teacher is a resource person who provides opportunities and materials for students. The teacher is a facilitator. Sometimes the teacher's role is to step back and learn from students as they engage in an activity. At other times the teacher asks the probing question that extends students' thinking. The teacher responds to writers about particular pieces, or talks to readers about what they are reading. The teacher uses knowledge about language and learning and an understanding of each student to keep the community of learners active and flourishing.

■ What about Reading Materials?

As a resource person the teacher makes available reading material from a variety of sources, including textbooks, trade books, newspapers, magazines, and references. These print materials enrich and enhance the curriculum by encouraging multiple and varied presentations of the subject matter. The uses of multiple texts allows and encourages choices, classroom collaboration, and diversity in modes of presentation. It avoids the notion that there is one "correct answer" from a single source.

Another important source of reading materials is the students' own writing, which may be in the form of learning logs, journals, reports, stories, poems, plays, or essays. Here students can respond, react, question, draw conclusions, and synthesize information. Reading and discussing the works of others reaffirms reading and writing as social acts performed by a community of learners.

■ What about Instructional Management/Essential Elements Systems?

Instructional management systems are curricular packages structured on the premise that all students in a given classroom need to go through the same materials in the same sequence to develop their language and learning. Such systems imply that all children grow as language users at the same pace and should use the same materials—and we know that this is incorrect. In these systems teachers are given sets of skills to be pretested, taught, and post-tested for every learner. The ignoring of individual differences becomes problematic for both students and teachers.

One of the hallmarks of a whole language program is that curricular decisions are based on the knowledge and needs of individual students. It is the teacher, not the instructional management developer, who has access to this knowledge. Therefore it is the teacher's professional responsibility to find the best strategy lessons and materials that will help each student become a better reader, writer, speaker, and listener. Whole language teaching is a viable alternative to pre-packaged curricular systems.

■ What about Evaluation?

In a whole language classroom evaluation emerges as a natural outgrowth of the curriculum. The evaluation is informal and continuous. Curricular decisions in a whole language classroom are based on careful, informed observation of students and the learner's own self-evaluation. Such decisions concern the cognitive, emotional, and social well-being of the student and are not derived from isolated performances on one or two tests. Evaluation begins by identifying the learner's strengths and areas of concern. Only then can the teacher develop and collect materials and strategy lessons that use the strengths of the learner to address these concerns.

Observing and describing are two sides of the same coin. Together they are called "kidwatching" (Y. Goodman, 1978). Observing can take place in the classroom, the hallway, the gym, the cafeteria, the library, or outside the school building. It may involve a call to students' parents to discover their impressions of how students are doing. General impressions of the students' efforts, successes, understandings, or misunderstandings are richer when viewed in several settings. These impressions are described in anecdotal records, journals, and learning logs, or are recorded on a teacher-made form. More specific evaluation can be done by observing students' reading and writing, noting behaviors within those processes, and then evaluating the written work.

Following observation and description, analysis involves coordinating general impressions, descriptive records, notes taken concerning student collaboration, and students' work. As the teacher reviews this documentation, patterns begin to emerge. The student may be reluctant to read in reading class, but eager to read the sports page from the newspaper during study hall. That teacher may wish to use that interest in the classroom by bringing in more sports materials for Sustained Silent Reading. Another student may be eager to read, but may dislike writing. A call home may confirm that this student has never felt successful with writing. The teacher needs to think of ways to extend the student's successful reading experience into a successful writing experience.

Evaluation becomes much more than grades on a report card or a pupil progress report at mid-quarter. Through ongoing evaluation the teacher finds out if a unit is successful, if students are understanding certain concepts and applying their knowledge in other situations. Kidwatching suggests the direction the class might take.

Students are our best informants. We can find out what they know and think by asking them questions such as: "What do you already know about this?" "What do you need to know?" "How can I help you?" "What did you learn?" "What do you still have questions about?" "What could you have done better?" This kind of self-evaluation is highly reliable. However, students must learn that they do not need questions from the teacher to self-evaluate. Bringing reading and writing to conscious awareness in the classroom encourages students to "think about thinking" (metacognition).

■ How Will Implementing a Whole Language Classroom Influence My Students' Scores on Standardized Tests?

This issue has been a major concern for many teachers who have implemented whole language programs. Though there is a great difference between the knowledge of discrete skills required on standardized tests (especially for younger students) and the processes of reading, writing, speaking, and listening for authentic purposes, students in whole language classrooms typically do as well on standardized tests as do students from classrooms where they spend a good deal of time drilling these skills.

Conversely, students who have practiced the types of isolated skills that are assessed on standardized tests do not necessarily perform those skills more successfully than do students from whole language classes. Why is this so?

Students in whole language classes use all the systems of language and all the contextual and cultural cues to make meaning when they are reading. They understand that there are many different strategies to employ in making meaning. Therefore they often use more of their repertoire of strategies when reading the artificial, contrived texts in most standardized tests. Though there are many ways to respond to test items, students drilled in discrete skills may not have the same array of meaning-making strategies, and may not possess the flexibility called for in standardized testing situations.

It is important to note that standardized tests are limiting in that they do not allow students to exhibit what they know and can do. To allow for easy test administration, test-makers use multiple-choice questions that narrow options and reduce and direct all thinking toward one "correct" answer. Because whole language classrooms emphasize open-ended questions, multiple answers, and problem-solving it is appropriate to assume the score on a standardized test to be a *minimum*, not a maximum, measure of what a student knows.

■ Will This Curriculum Greatly Increase My Workload?

In a whole language classroom not everything the students write is taken to final form and then graded; not everything read is to be pre-taught, read, and then tested. Not all knowledge shared becomes objectives met. If one defines work as correcting mounds of worksheets and tests, monitoring mastery of objectives, and other copious record-keeping devices—then a whole language curriculum would mean a *reduced* workload.

If "work" is defined as watching, listening, and getting to know students; gathering and providing appropriate materials; offering learning opportunities; and organizing an active community of learners—then this curriculum does require a fair amount of work. However, the work is professional, creative, and exciting. The satisfaction for both teacher and learners tends to make the work less important than the results.

■ Is Whole Language Only a Matter of Using Certain Procedures?

Whole language classroom practices and procedures reflect a consistent set of beliefs about language, learning, and teaching. Whole language teachers share classroom strategy lessons and theoretical beliefs such as those discussed in Chapter 1. By observing learners and testing hypotheses about these observations, theory and practice merge.

In *What's Whole in Whole Language?* (1986) Kenneth Goodman points out that an important characteristic of whole language teaching is commitment. Even though teaching is a process, teachers tend to become preoccupied by the outcomes, results, or products of teaching. Whole language teachers establish, examine, and continually refine their teaching based on the abilities and needs of learners.

■ How Does One Get Started in Whole Language Teaching?

> Whole language is clearly a lot of things to a lot of people; it's not a dogma to be narrowly practiced. It's a way of bringing together a view of language, a view of learning, and a view of people, in particular two special groups of people: kids and teachers (K. Goodman, 1986, p. 5).

Ken Goodman's words are empowering. Teachers, like students, grow and develop through learning. Whole language instruction means that teachers:

Learn from kids. Begin by becoming enlightened observers of your students; learn how much they know and can do.
Collaborate. Work with students and develop strategy lessons that will meet students' individual needs.
Seek and disseminate. Shared theory and practice tend to bring teachers together. Whole language teachers seem to find one another within their schools, in their communities, throughout their states, and across the country. Attend in-service workshops or professional conferences to meet others and share ideas. Whole language teaching is sustained and nurtured by teacher support.
Read and imagine. As you continue to read this book and as you select and read additional sources, imagine the possibilities.

References for Part I

Camus, A. (1948). *The plague* (S. Gilbert, trans.). N.Y.: Modern Library.

Goodman, K. (1986). *What's whole in whole language?* Portsmouth, NH: Heinemann.

Goodman, Y. (1978). Kid watching: An alternative to testing. *Journal of National Elementary Principals, 57* (4), 41–45.

Gollasch, F. (ed.). (1982). *Language and literacy: The selected writings of Kenneth S. Goodman, Vols. 1 & 2.* Boston: Routledge and Kegan Paul.

Graves, D. (1978). Balance the basics: Let them write. *Learning,* April, 30–33.

Harste, J., and Burke, C. (1977). A new hypothesis for reading teacher research: Both teaching and learning of reading are theoretically based. In P. D. Pearson (ed.), *Reading: Theory, Research and Practice, 26th Yearbook of the National Reading Conference.* St. Paul, MN: Mason.

Harste, J., Pierce, K., and Cairney, T. (eds.). (1985). *The authoring cycle: A viewing guide.* Portsmouth, NH: Heinemann.

Harste, J., Woodward, V., and Burke, C. (1984). *Language Stories & Literacy Lessons.* Portsmouth, NH: Heinemann.

Karty, J. (director). (1981). *The autobiography of Ms. Jane Pittman.* [Film]. N.Y.: RCA.

Neisser, U. (1976). *Cognition and reality.* San Francisco: W.H. Freeman.

Orwell, G. (1949). *1984.* N.Y.: Harcourt.

Seuss, Dr. (1971). *The Lorax.* N.Y.: Random House.

Smith, F. (1973). *Psycholinguistics and reading.* N.Y.: Holt, Rinehart and Winston.

Smith, F. (1979). *Reading without nonsense.* N.Y.: Teachers College Press of Columbia University.

Watson, D. (October 1986.). Whole language classrooms. Paper presented at meeting of Teachers Applying Whole Language, Columbia, MO.

PART II

Strategy Lessons

4

General Strategy Lessons

All of the strategy lessons in this book are grounded in the belief that learning is purposeful. A "general" strategy lesson is a learning experience that is appropriate and applicable in many settings; it is used with various combinations of individuals and groups. A strategy lesson is an invitation to help learners interact with language in meaningful ways. These lessons assist individuals with specific needs or help groups of students use reading, writing, listening, and speaking as tools for learning concepts in various content fields.

The purpose of introducing and demonstrating general strategy lessons is that students can apply and use the strategies as their own aids to learning. The ideas presented range from a focus on individuals' dealing directly with text to peer group collaboration for sharing and expanding understanding. Strategy lessons for the individual include "Sustained Silent Reading" (4.1), "Starting Strategy Lesson for Writing Response/Reactions" (4.5), "Pursuit of Truth" (4.7), "REAP Procedure" (4.8), "ERRQ" (4.10), and "ERRQ + R" (4.11). These meet individual needs in group settings.

Many strategy lessons are demonstrated in a group setting for individuals to use independently and with others. Such strategy lessons include: "Re Quest" (4.9), "Prove It" (4.14), and "Ask Something" (4.12). "Peer Partners in Learning" (4.15) provides good background for understanding the other strategy lessons that use peer assistance, such as "Shotgunning" (4.16). You will notice that many of the strategy lessons presented combine a number of other activities. Such "hybrids" evolve when ideas are consolidated. Other strategy lessons provide complementary activities, as is the case with "Autobiographies" (4.19) and "I Know What You Mean" (4.20).

Whether a strategy lesson focuses on individual or group needs, all learning is social. The following strategy lessons suggest opportunities for students to work independently or collaboratively within accessible and varied social contexts.

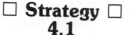

Sustained Silent Reading

Adapted from R. McCracken

Why?

This strategy lesson provides a daily uninterrupted silent time for pleasure reading by students and teachers. It promotes positive attitudes toward reading.

Who?

All students and teachers will benefit from having time to read independently for pleasure. Not only is it an enjoyable activity, but it also provides an opportunity to practice the skill of reading in a pressure-free situation.

How?

1. Each student and the teacher read silently. This is not the time to read homework assignments or to grade papers but a time to read something for enjoyment.
2. No interruptions are permitted. You might say, "I'm really involved in this, please do not interrupt me." This helps to demonstrate to students that this is an important activity.
3. Each student selects or brings a book, magazine, or newspaper to read. No book changing takes place during reading time. Have a wide variety of materials available for selection. For the student who is reluctant to choose, the teacher or other students can help (see Strategy 9.1, "Ways to Help Students Find 'Just the Right Book' ").
4. A timer is used and should be placed where no one can see it so all can read without considering the time. When the timer rings, anyone who needs to may continue until reaching a good stopping place.
5. There are absolutely no reports or records of any kind required, although discussions and informal response writing are optional as they naturally evolve. Many students enjoy sharing what they have read. The teacher can demonstrate this activity.

Then What?

1. Sustained Silent Reading should be done on a regular basis. Some teachers set aside time to read each day. One class period per week can be devoted to the activity. Some schools have a Sustained Silent Reading time for the whole building. Consistency and predictability will help establish the habit of reading for fun.
2. Content area classes can have Sustained Silent Reading time to read books that students choose (historical fiction in social studies, for example) related to that content area.

Skinny Books

Adapted from D. Watson

Why?

The process of constructing meaning involves a combination of sampling from the linguistic cues in the text and the background and experiences of the learner. When the conceptual load of a text is too great, the reader needs the support of a supplementary text to build concepts that expand the background and experience.

Who?

Students who need to bridge the gap between existing knowledge and the concepts presented in a given text will benefit from this activity.

How?

1. Act as a previewer, author, and collector of materials to provide alternative texts for building concepts. Preview the content of the text and make a list of concepts that appear difficult.
2. Materials are collected from alternative texts, trade books, magazines, or other sources to provide help in explaining concepts. If printed sources are inadequate, write a short passage to provide the needed information.
3. A "Skinny Book" is a short book that deals with one concept. For example, if the assigned topic is local elections, one Skinny Book can include newspaper clippings that report the qualifications of the local candidates. Another Skinny Book can address the rules of voting. A sample ballot can be the subject of a third book.
4. Provide time for students to read and discuss the supplementary texts. This time is valuable for clarification of concepts and the sharing of ideas.
5. Present the assigned text and encourage students to apply the shared information gained from the smaller texts.

Then What?

After demonstrating the activity students can participate from the very beginning. They can preview, list difficult concepts, and create or collect materials for making their own Skinny Books.

Other possibilities for Skinny Books are: discarded textbooks; magazine features or stories; notes from films, television, or guest speakers; or students' own research. Simple covers can be made from cardboard, construction paper, and contact paper.

Let's Get Started

Adapted from A. V. Manzo's "Guided Reading Procedure"

Why?

This strategy lesson enhances recall through the use of implicit questions, organization, and written responses to reading material. It utilizes material relevant to the students' content area classes; and it is also valuable for encouraging group discussion.

Who?

Students who experience difficulty in understanding and retelling their textbook materials will benefit from this strategy.

How?

1. You and your students read the same passage and then turn the book face down. The students offer all ideas they can retell from the passage and record these ideas in abbreviated form. These ideas are discussed for additions and corrections. This procedure guides unaided retelling.
2. The students compare their retellings to the original passage. They reread for clarification of points, and add to or delete from their original retellings. This aids the recognition of implicit questions.
3. After students are satisfied that they have retold the passage, they organize the information into a response. A response includes both retelling and reaction. It may take the form of sequence pattern, web, diagram, or outline.
4. Ask thoughtful, open-ended questions to aid fullest understanding of the passage. For example: "Can you tell me more?" "What does this remind you of?" "What would you have done?"

   Post-reading summary writing is preferable to answering objective-type test questions.

Written Conversation

Adapted from C. Burke

Why?

The communicative component of writing is sometimes difficult for writers to perceive because of the distance of the audience. This strategy lesson brings author and readers together in a transactive process in which feedback in the way of response and questioning is immediately available to the writer. This type of writing experience is personal and takes place in a meaningful social context.

Who?

Written Conversation (Burke, cited in Harste, 1985) can be used in all grade levels and content areas. The flexibility of this activity makes it a valuable component of any topic of study. Because each participant takes an active role, this activity is especially helpful for reluctant writers.

How?

The class divides into groups (usually pairs or triads). Each person has paper and a pencil or pen. The members of the group carry on a conversation in writing; no talking is allowed. Students can share their writing with other students if they wish. Anything that can be discussed verbally can be discussed in a Written Conversation.

Then What?

The following are variations on Written Conversation and can be used in a variety of settings with almost any grade level or content area.

1. Students find partners and choose a short story that they both want to read. After reading:
   a. Each person writes about important events in the story and something about the main characters.
   b. Students switch papers and read their partner's retelling.
   c. In Written Conversations the students write questions and comments back and forth about the story and about the retelling.
2. You and the students discuss what they are reading in a Written Conversation.
3. Private discussions can take place in the classroom using Written Conversation. [Note: If you are concerned that "inappropriate" topics will be discussed, the students need to know that whether or not any Written Conversation is collected, they are subject to your scrutiny.]
4. A Written Conversation format can be used as a warm-up or prewriting activity for a play, skit, or sketch.
5. In content area classes use Written Conversation as a review technique at the beginning or ending of a class unit, or as a clarifying strategy for any concepts or content.

Starting Strategy Lesson for Writing Response/Reactions

Adapted from "Clustering" by G. Rico

Why?

This clustering strategy lesson encourages students to write response/reactions, which generate ideas, form insights about the reading material, and create connections and relationships. This technique can be used with any type of writing—journals, letters, essays, poetry, fiction, and nonfiction.

Who?

All students will benefit from making personal connections between what they read and their own lives, especially the reluctant writer.

How?

1. After reading any fiction or nonfiction, students think of a phrase or a word that illustrates their reactions to the text. They can react to anything: themes, characters, events, and so on. This initial reaction is the starting point, the nucleus. Students put this nucleus reaction in a circle in the center of their papers.
2. Encourage students to "let go" and flow with the current of connections that come into their heads. They write these words or phrases down, radiating out from the nucleus, connecting them to the nucleus and each other with lines. These connections lead to other associations.
3. After students have spent a few minutes making associations they write vignettes based on these associations. They are selective in the associations they choose to write about.
4. If students have difficulty identifying the difference between cluster words that retell the story and those that tell how they respond to the story, reaction words can be highlighted with a colored pen. They can also circle the words that make connections to another idea in different colors.

Demystifying Textbooks, or
Now What Do I Do?

By M. Bixby

Why?

This activity enables students to set a purpose for reading, to make decisions about time constraints, and to use the background experiences that they bring to the texts. It helps them create hypothetical situations for their classmates to discuss.

Who?

Students who read and reread chapters in their books and still feel that they do not comprehend the material will benefit from this activity.

How?

1. Students should be familiar with various reading stategies, including skimming for important information and scanning for details.
2. Distribute the "Selective Reading" questionnaire (see below), and have students answer the questions. It is important for them to annotate and justify their answers, making references to the passages.
3. Students discuss their answers in small groups. They will have many opinions concerning how to handle reading situations.
4. Provide time for students to create and exchange their reading surveys. They will be writing from their own experiences, and suggestions and strategies from their peers will be helpful. All students have varied reading situations to share.
5. Share the strategies in the large group. Ask probing questions to clarify issues and to cause the students to consider their strategies.

Then What?

This activity can initiate a "consciousness raising" session for the students. It affords them the opportunity to talk about problem classes, books that are giving them difficulty, and strategies that they are using. They can offer each other useful advice based on their own experiences. It's good fun to listen in.

Selective Reading

Each of the statements below describes a reading situation and the material to be read. Read each item and decide whether you should:

A. Read the material carefully and completely.
B. Read parts and skip parts.
C. Skip most of the material; read for specific details.
D. Other strategies; your choice (explain).

1. You are reading an historical novel assigned as a supplement to an American history class. Your instructor suggested you read it to understand

better what it was like to live prior to the outbreak of the American Revolution. You come to a long, detailed section on the architecture of the period. How should you read the section? _____

2. You are reading a chapter in economics. You know you will have a quiz on it next week, and the quizzes are always very thorough. How should you read the chapter? _____

3. You are studying a chapter on genetics that you read two weeks ago for a comprehensive final exam next week. You have already had a quiz over this chapter, for which you received 9 out of 15 as a correct score. How should you read the chapter? _____

4. You are doing a research paper for political science on U.S. presidential elections. You have found a fairly lengthy but very interesting book on the history of elections up to 1900. How should you read the book? _____

5. You have just attended an English class in which the instructor lectured on *Paradise Lost* and made important references to the Bible. You are not familiar with the Bible and didn't recognize the references. You decide it is important to know about the Bible. How should you read it? _____

6. Tomorrow you will be attending a lecture in biology about the nervous system of vertebrates. You feel that you don't know anything about the subject or the terminology. How should you read the chapter in the text? _____

7. Your psychology instructor gave your class a list of fifteen terms taken from a chapter in the book. You are expected to know them for a lab quiz tomorrow. How should you read the chapter? _____

8. You have been procrastinating for three weeks, and you have an essay test tomorrow over six chapters from your art history text. How should you read the chapters? _____

9. You received a "D" on your first anthropology exam. When you reviewed the test, you discovered that you had studied the wrong material for it. You expected the test to be over the lectures, and nearly all the questions were on the material in the text or from the assigned paperback. Your next exam is in ten days. How should you be reading your books? _____

10. Your lecturer in chemistry thinks everything she says is terribly important. She also wrote the textbook, and her lectures follow the chapters very closely. She even uses the same examples on the board. When studying for next week's exam, how should you read the book? _____

Pursuit of Truth: Four Questions to Promote Active Reading of Nonfiction

By D. Pyle

Why?

Part of active reading is the pursuit of answers to questions. Comprehension is enhanced when learners formulate their own questions and use these to monitor their understanding of texts. High-school students who have had a lot of experience using the organizational features of textbooks are sometimes confused about how to approach nonfiction pieces that are not packaged in textbook format. The guidelines for active reading that follow can help students develop strategies for approaching and responding to unfamiliar nonfiction.

Who?

Secondary students who need experience in reading nonfiction will benefit from this activity.

How?

1. Review the importance of establishing a purpose for reading. Students share strategies they have developed on their own for dealing with unfamiliar or difficult information.
2. Present students with the following guidelines for active reading:

Four Basic Questions an Active Reader Asks

A. *What is the book (or article) about as a whole?* This question should be in the reader's mind before and during reading. It is posed in order to help readers discover the leading theme and to predict the author's treatment of that theme.
B. *What is being said in detail and how?* This question is asked before and during reading to help readers focus on the author's main points, assertions, and arguments.
C. *Does the book ring true in whole or part?* Keeping this question in mind during reading can help readers use personal experience to determine the author's intent and to judge the quality of the information communicated.
D. *What of it?* This question helps readers read "beyond the lines" and determine the significance of the information presented. This is the question that leads to further reading, oral discussion, or written response.

Then What?

1. Discuss with students how these four *general* questions can help them devise specific questions and learning strategies for various reading experiences. For example, to answer the first question the learner might decide to selectively read portions of a book or article to discover how the author's organization (style of writing, subheadings, illustrations, and so on) can be used to aid comprehension.

2. Suggest several short nonfiction articles for students to read. Ask them to use the four questions to guide their reading and suggest strategies. Students may want to write down their individually conceived questions before they begin to read. After reading they should answer their own questions in written responses.

3. Ask students to evaluate the effectiveness of the four questions and suggest modifications.

REAP Procedure

Adapted from A. V. Manzo

Why?

This strategy lesson is used to help students comprehend written materials and prepare for essay or short-answer exams. It helps them extract and organize important points from texts and translate ideas into their own words. The keys to the success of this procedure are the choice of relevant, interesting material and the teacher's thoughtful and careful demonstration of the procedure.

Who?

Students who wish to comprehend their textbooks better and organize their reading benefit from this strategy. It can be used successfully with individual students or small groups.

How?

The acronym REAP stands for:

Read the material—this may be a text chapter or part of one.
Encode—translate into your own words.
Annotate—make an overt response to the important ideas.
Ponder—think about and revise your annotation.

Follow these steps:

1. Everyone reads the selection.
2. Help students recognize and define the needed information or quote by discussing and giving examples.
3. Help students to discriminate between statements that are too broad or too narrow. This will help them to translate the passage into their own words.
4. Demonstrate an annotation. As you write it on the board or overhead "think aloud" and show students the process of annotation.
5. Students practice writing individually, then work together in small groups (two to five people), and compare their passages.

What kind of annotations might there be? Originally, there were seven kinds of annotations. However, some overlap. The seven can be reduced to the following five:

1. *Quote*—find a statement of the main issues in the author's own words.
2. *Thesis*—restate the major propositions of the passage.
3. *Summary*—usually a paragraph with the main idea of the passage together with important support ideas in additional sentences. Possible patterns for these paragraphs include chronology, spatial relationships, most-to-least, or least-to-most.
4. *Relationship summary*—ideas may fall into relationships, such as comparison/contrast, question/answer, problem/solution, or cause/effect. These are useful in recording important ideas, and they are easy to remember.
5. *Critical summary*—the support or rejection of what someone said; it may or may not include a major proposition or recapitulation.

Then What?

Another possibility is to have students write three annotations on one particular passage: one too brief to be of any value; one too long and overly detailed; and one that is well stated, direct, and contains the essential information.

Discussion

The order of the types of annotations reflects the increasing amount of difficulty, effort, and/or analytical thinking to create them. No one kind of annotation is "correct," though obviously some selections lend themselves more readily to certain kinds of annotations. Students need practice in deciding what sort of annotations are appropriate for their readings. They should make their judgments (if possible) before they begin to write, or certainly as they are writing, not as an afterthought. They should base their judgments on length, difficulty, and content of the material while also considering how they will be using the material in the classroom situation. It is interesting to let students read a passage, decide on a kind of annotation, write, and then compare the kinds and contents of their work with others.

ReQuest: Reciprocal Questioning

Adapted from A. V. Manzo

Why?

This strategy lesson encourages students to question as they read. Questioning helps readers to predict, to discover new meanings in texts, and to improve their comprehension.

Who?

This strategy lesson helps passive readers become active, questioning readers. Students who do not monitor their comprehension as they read will benefit from this activity.

How?

1. Choose a text that is a bit challenging for the student, either a story or a passage from a textbook.
2. Tell the student to read for understanding because you will exchange questions about the passage.
3. Each person reads the first paragraph silently. The student asks the teacher a question about the text. The question can be a "school question" (such as "What is the main idea of the paragraph?"), a recall question ("Who was the first person to sail around the world?"), a response question ("Did you like it?"), or a "real" question ("Why would someone do something like that?"). By being responsible for asking the first question the ownership of retelling is removed from the student and gives him or her control of the text. Demonstrate the process of comprehending by explaining the kinds of thinking processes that were involved in coming up with that particular answer.
4. Ask the student a question. The question should elicit a response based on textual information and must be one that the student can answer so that success is guaranteed, such as: "How would you feel if someone lied to you as the boy did in this paragraph?" This offers a demonstration of good questioning that the reader can begin to use in the strategy and, hopefully, in independent reading in the future.
5. Reciprocal questioning continues until the student has enough information to predict what might happen in the passage. At this point the student reads the story independently to check the prediction.

Then What?

1. ReQuest can be utilized with the entire class, using longer selections. The class tries to stump the teacher by asking difficult questions, and the teacher gets the same opportunity. Students begin to see that questions vary in quality, and they can observe questioning behavior in others.
2. This strategy can be used as a Written Conversation (see Strategy 4.4).

ERRQ

By D. Watson and C. Gilles

Why?

Readers who make a commitment to the text and try to link new information to their own background experiences are more likely to get meaning from the text. Questioning enables students to frame what they know in a new context and gives the teacher a way to understand the reader's comprehension better.

Who?

Students who give up easily when reading, students who do not personalize information from the text, and those who have difficulty asking and answering probing questions will benefit from this strategy lesson.

How?

1. Explain that ERRQ stands for:

   Estimate
   Read
   Respond
   Question

   Students look over a selection they choose to read and estimate how far they can read it with understanding. How far can they stay with the text? The students mark the place lightly in pencil or record the page number.
2. Students are urged to consider how the text is making them feel, and if any images come to mind as they read. Does the text remind them of anything from their lives? Students read the text silently, orally, or with a partner in paired reading.
3. After reading, students react. What came to mind as they read the article? Did images or memories flash in their minds? How did it make them feel? After reacting, the students retell everything they can remember about the article.
4. Students ask at least two questions about the reading. The questions can range from "What was the main idea?" to "How will the book end?" or "Why was it so sad?"

Then What?

1. Students can respond and question orally or in writing, depending on the size of the group, the age of the students, and the purpose.
2. Students can select their own reading material or, in content classes, the teacher can select the materials.
3. The reaction portion of the response can lead naturally into retelling. Many students begin reacting and end up retelling. Usually, the better the reaction, the better the retelling. Depending on the quality of the reaction and the teacher's purpose, the retelling need not be done every time.

4. The questioning portion can be modified. If students have difficulty asking questions as they read, the teacher can share questions with them. If questioning is a written activity, the questions can serve as the beginning of a dialogue or Written Conversations (see Strategy 4.4) between you and the students.

ERRQ + R (Remember)

By S. R. Crenshaw

Why?

ERRQ is an effective strategy lesson to guide students in making a commitment to understanding text (see Strategy 4.10). This is an extension of that strategy to assist in recalling information.

Who?

Students who need assistance in adapting or developing experiences in recalling information.

How?

This follows the use of the ERRQ strategy:

Estimate—students estimate the volume of print they can read and comprehend in a given time period.
Read—they read the selected passage.
React/Reflect—they react to the ideas presented in writing or orally.
Question—they formulate questions relevant to the material.

1. Collect the questions after the students have had an opportunity to share them with others in the class.
2. At the next class session students write *I remember . . .* on a sheet of paper and list all the facts or ideas that they can remember from the previous reading material. Set a time limit that is appropriate for the class (two to five minutes).
3. Return the individual questions and ask students to check the items listed that are related to the questions they composed earlier.
4. Initiate a discussion to share the results. Some guiding questions include:

   Did your list match most of your questions?
   How much did the questions help in remembering the material?
   Did you include extra information that was not covered in your questions?
   What is the purpose of creating questions based on reading material?
   What did you learn from this activity?*

Then What?

This strategy lesson can be adapted to other situations and events. It has worked best in content areas that require the retention of factual information. The strategy was designed to help students see the possibilities of extending study strategies. The major objective is that they use what is most helpful for them in developing personalized learning.

*A perceptive student's reply to this question: "Well, I learned that you gotta know a lot more to ask questions than you do to answer them."

Ask Something

By P. Crowley

Why?

Teachers often encourage students to improve their first writing drafts by making them more concise, descriptive, and interesting. This can be done through demonstration or through notes jotted in the margin of students' papers. Students learn from teachers, but they also learn from their peers. Learners can help each other move ahead in their writing ability with a minimum of help from the teacher.

Who?

Students who need to become more aware of their audiences when evaluating their written work for revision will benefit from this strategy lesson. It is also helpful to writers who need direction for reworking the structure and reconsidering the content of the first draft.

How?

1. After you and the students have written on topics of interest, pass your papers to the next person in your group.
2. Each person reads the paper and writes at least one question that they think needs to be addressed in the paper.
3. After the questions have been asked, the paper is passed on to the next person for the same purpose. When the members of the groups have asked their questions, the papers are returned to the authors.
4. Revising the first story involves reading the questions posed by other members of the group and rewriting the original story, incorporating the answers to the questions in an appropriate place in the story. The authors choose which questions need to be answered to improve their stories.

Then What?

1. Partners can read each other's papers, discuss their improvement from the first draft, and make additional suggestions.
2. More than one question can be asked by members of the group.
3. Questions that were particularly helpful to a writer can be shared with the class and discussed.
4. After writers have asked each other questions, they can generate their own questions for their own writings.

Using Context to Develop Meaning

Adapted from Y. Goodman and C. Burke by C. Collins

Why?

Reading involves the integrated use of all the cueing systems—the symbol-sound relationships, grammar, meaning, and off-the-page (pragmatic) cues. This strategy lesson helps the reader focus on meaning cues.

Who?

Students who concentrate only on print and don't read for meaning will benefit from this activity. Readers who make some use of context clues within the sentence but not in the whole text will also benefit.

How?

1. Tell students that they will be reading a text in which there may be an unknown concept. Students are challenged to try to figure out the concept by reading the passage (see example below). It is important to choose a text that provides clear contextual clues to the meaning of the concept.
2. Using the board or an overhead projector, reveal the first sentence of the text. Students predict the meaning of the unknown concept. Each of these predictions is written on the board. Reveal the second sentence and eliminate the first predictions that students agree are no longer appropriate with this new information and add any new predictions. Continue with this procedure until the text is completed.
3. Discuss the process that the class went through to understand the unfamiliar concept. What helped from the text? Was anything confusing? When were you sure you knew the meaning?
4. Students are encouraged to use this strategy as they read independently and to share with the class examples of the process of comprehending unfamiliar concepts.

   Thanks to the abruptness of his forced landing, he didn't have to search for a walking stick. There was an abundance of shattered splintered limbs strewn in the fighter's wake. He selected one which would serve both for support and for testing the ground ahead.

   Using the nose of the ship as a crude guide, he set his *tracomp* and they started off, angling a few degrees to starboard. . . .

   Nonetheless, he now had to direct all his attention to keeping to his predetermined path. Despite the *tracomp* built into his suit sleeve he knew he could easily lose his way. A deviation of a tenth of a degree could be critical.*

Then What?

1. This activity can be used in small groups or pairs. Students can also make individual predictions and discuss these after the text is totally revealed.

2. Students can play a game of "Who am I?" or "What am I?"—giving clues that progress from broad to specific. These games can be written and exchanged. Clues can be written on one side of a card and pictures of the "who" or the "what" can be drawn on the other side. These cards can be useful in the content areas for building concept background, similar to "Skinny Books" (see Strategy 4.2).

*From Alan Foster's *Splinter of the Mind's Eye,* pages 13–14.

Prove It

By M. Bixby

Why?

Summary writing is a good assessment of reading comprehension, as well as a facilitator of it. In order for students to write good summaries they must have a sense of what is important in what they are reading. A partner's reaction to a summary can be helpful in editing the author's response. The best summaries are those that are written in the students' own words, evaluated in light of the original text, and edited for richer meaning.

Who?

Any student will find this strategy lesson useful for reading literature, expository prose, or textbooks.

How?

1. Partners find a text or texts to read, then:

    Predict—important points from a preview of the text. Students may or may not write their predictions. The predictions set purposes for reading.

    Read—to confirm, build on, or alter predictions. Students read for the main ideas and to summarize in their own words.

    Organize—important ideas made into a response. A response includes a retelling of text-contingent information and a reaction to that information. Reactions relate the author's ideas to the students' background experiences (see Strategy 4.9). Up to this point, each student is working alone. When each is finished, summaries are exchanged.

    Validate—partner's ideas are validated and partners are asked to verify—"I don't remember that the author said that; it's misinformation; prove it!" In some way mark the parts of the summary checked in the original, or discuss.

    After partners validate and verify to each other's satisfaction, each is to:

    Edit—original summary is edited, taking cues from their partners, improving both the form and content.

Then What?

1. Have partners pick and read different pieces of text, but exchange and evaluate each other's summaries. One student may work on history, while another picks science. It is interesting to see how students' lack of exposure to the texts would change their responses to their partner's summaries. Would they ask for more verification or less because they'd not read the passage?

2. Students will eventually see that they can spot concerns in summaries and write good questions for their partners without prior knowledge of partners' texts. "You don't have to know the answers to write good questions if you're a good predictor!"

When students become comfortable with this activity, they will find summarizing a welcome aid to their comprehension. In addition, they will see that their edited summaries are more useful for studying than are the original texts, because one's own language is more meaningful than the often inconsiderate language of the texts.

Peer Partners in Learning: Classroom Collaboration

By R. Steffes and G. Grupe

Why?

Learning is socially motivated. When students are encouraged to help one another, each grows academically and socially. Classroom collaboration involves matching two students who can work together and help each other in class. Students can influence their peers by helping them look "a head taller" in learning situations, and helping them avoid potential problems.

Who?

All students will benefit from engaging in collaborative learning, particularly students who are having difficulty in school.

How?

Knowledge of students' abilities and personalities is helpful in suggesting peer-partnerships because these partnerships will change depending on the topics and the students' knowledge.

Some possible matches are:

1. Pair students according to their backgrounds and experiences with the topic being studied. The more knowledgeable student acts as tutor, giving individual explanations, assignment descriptions, and so on. This provides the student with the opportunity to describe, organize, and explain. The other student often becomes more motivated, learns to ask probing questions, and learns more about the specific subject.
2. Match one student proficient in oral communication with another proficient in written communication. The pair produces joint oral and written projects, each learning from the other. This results in students having more self-confidence and better attitudes toward school.

Then What?

Regardless of who is matched up in the classroom, students have the opportunity to set and meet their own goals. These goals might include:

1. At the beginning of the class period check with your partner to see if he or she has the appropriate materials and is ready to begin class.
2. During the hour occasionally double-check (through observation or quiet discussion) to see that each is contributing to the class, understanding the information, and taking appropriate notes.
3. At the end of the hour partners check that homework assignments are written down and that each partner leaves the room with appropriate materials.

Shotgunning, or Collaborative Reading

By M. Bixby

Why?

Students often mistakenly believe that they should handle all reading assignments by themselves. By collaborating, students become more responsible for their parts of a group project. Students can also become more active readers by sharing their reading and study strategies.

Who?

This strategy lesson is designed for secondary and post-secondary students who are enrolled in the same content area classes and have the same reading assignments.

How?

1. Begin with an analogy that explains the title of the activity: Collaborative reading is like a shotgun blast in that it is quick, intense, covers a lot of territory, and is therefore highly effective.
2. Students divide into pairs or small groups and each is responsible for reading a section of the target text (which may be a textbook chapter, a magazine article, part of a novel, and so on).
3. Group members decide how to divide the text and how they will record their portions. Methods of recording include a summary, outline, drawing, or any visual representation.
4. Groups agree on time limits for their individual reading and information-gathering.
5. After students finish, they decide on ways to consolidate their information. Strategies for consolidation include:

   Each student discusses a section and others take notes.
   Group members copy each other's sketches or writing.
   Photocopies of each part are distributed.
   Group members interview each other about different sections.

Then What?

1. As a class, students discuss their strategies for dividing and consolidating the readings.
2. Groups compose possible questions to ask each other about the readings.
3. Groups can do further reading on their subject.
4. Groups can meet again to discuss their topics further.

Views and Interviews

By S. R. Crenshaw

Why?

This activity is designed to encourage questioning strategies; to develop creative thinking; and to provide the means for integrating language competencies in listening, speaking, writing, and reading.

Who?

Students who have had little practice with interviewing and/or those who are reticent to ask questions will benefit from this activity.

How?

1. Generate a discussion concerning television interviews and opinion polls. Encourage students to give their opinions about a few topics of their choice.
2. Brainstorm some possible questions that would give the desired information and write these on the board or on a large piece of paper. Students choose the three or four "best" questions and write them on their papers. Suggest working in pairs or small groups to develop other pertinent questions.
3. Choose a student and demonstrate appropriate interview questioning techniques. Then students practice interviewing one another, avoiding questions which elicit only "yes" or "no" responses.
4. After the interviews the class discusses the questions: Which ones elicited sparse responses? Which drew out the interviewees? What questions could have been asked as "follow-ups"?
5. Suggest that individuals develop their own questions about a topic, make arrangements to interview five persons, and bring back the results for class analysis. Some basic statistical analysis may be used, if appropriate.
6. Students can use categorization or graphing to record results. If the polls or interviews are of general interest, students may wish to publish the results in the classroom or school newspaper.

Then What?

1. Interviewing can be used in content areas where students focus on current events or individual interests.
2. Students can study two or three different television commentators and note the types of questions that get the best responses.

Switching Roles

By P. Crowley

Why?

Rather than always receiving information in the classroom, learners need opportunities to present what they know. When students share knowledge and experiences with others, their own understanding is clarified and sharpened.

Who?

Language is a social event, and all language users will benefit by sharing experiences with their peers.

How?

1. This strategy lesson involves students teaching the class. Begin by discussing the notion of the classroom partnership, including cooperation, respect, and the fact that everyone is an expert on some topic.
2. Students choose any topic (within appropriate boundaries) that they would like to teach. They can have an entire period or any part of one. The students are responsible for preparing a lesson plan, taking care of any class "business" (such as attendance), and carrying out the lesson. The lesson can take the form of a lecture, reading and informal discussion, group work, or any other structure the student chooses. Any materials that need to be reproduced are turned in to the teacher the day before the student's lesson. The teacher becomes a student and takes part in the lesson as any other students would. This offers the teacher an opportunity to demonstrate questioning and note-taking.

Then What?

1. Time is available for the student, as teacher, to follow-up the activities.
2. Students teach in a specific content area.
3. Two or more students may present together.

Autobiographies of Language Users

By M. Bixby

Why?

Learners need opportunities to examine their pasts as readers, writers, speakers, and listeners both in and out of school. Through exploring their pasts, students can understand their current practices and attitudes toward language and learning. The impact of new learning experiences may be contingent upon recognizing or rethinking past experiences with language.

Who?

All students, particularly older ones, will benefit from reflecting on their experiences as language users.

How?

1. Students think about their pasts as readers, writers, speakers, and/or listeners in school and out. They remember (think a while before writing) a time in their lives or a person in their lives: a school year; a class; an event; a particular assignment or text; a certain teacher, friend, or relative.
2. They describe that event, situation, and/or person that had a good or bad impact on them, and they begin to focus on some phenomenon that contributed to who they are today.
3. Be sure students address questions such as: "What happened that caused you to use language in the way(s) that you do? How do you feel about this phenomenon now?"
4. Students write as long as they need to in order to fully describe and reflect upon that part of their lives. They may discover something about themselves that they weren't aware of before.

Then What?

1. After students think and write they can exchange their drafts with partners and move into "Ask Something" (see Strategy 4.2) or "Written Conversation" (see Strategy 4.4) in order to enhance their pieces.
2. The autobiographies can be organized into a class book, which can be illustrated with photos of influential people or with samples of students' early writing.
3. Excerpts from the writings can be used for the companion activity, "I Know What You Mean" (see Strategy 4.20).

I Know What You Mean

By M. Bixby

Why?

In order to take the risks necessary to change and improve their learning strategies, students should understand their previous learning experiences, both positive and negative. Students need to understand that they have school experiences in common with classmates.

Who?

All students benefit from responding to past schooling and learning experiences of their peers.

How?

1. Prior to this lesson students have written autobiographies of themselves as language users (see Strategy 4.19). These writings focus on the influence of some event or person on their lives in terms of their growth as readers, writers, speakers, and listeners.
2. Distribute pages of excerpts from previously written student autobiographies. These excerpts should address a diverse range of issues—for example, the impact of testing; an influential teacher, friend, or relative; learning to read and write; playing school; learning about ethnic or other individual differences; and so on.
3. Students read all the excerpts, then pick three or four to which they will write responses. Each response is written to the author of the excerpt as though the writer were speaking directly to the other student.

Then What?

1. After writing, students can discuss the excerpts they found to be most interesting or most similar to their own experiences.
2. Students can share their own past language experiences in and out of school.

5

Graphic Organizers

Readers use numerous strategies that assist them in processing information before, during, and after reading. Teachers are familiar with outlining, advance organizers, charts, graphs, and categorizing as visual aids to organizing materials. Graphic organizers have several names and forms, depending on the context. Various graphic organizers are used to predict, explore, and expand learners' concepts. All of these activities may be used in the process of previewing and reviewing reading material. They are certainly appropriate for any content area. Illustrating the relationship of ideas can be accomplished through schematic diagrams, outlines, clustering, semantic webbing, and strategy lessons such as "Sketch to Stretch" (Strategy 5.4).

The following strategies are included to provide ideas that may be adapted in specific situations. This section highlights the notion that learners utilize a variety of strategies for categorizing and comprehending information.

Semantic Webbing

By S. R. Crenshaw

Why?

It is important to elicit prior knowledge and establish background information to build student understanding in any subject area. Understanding what students already know helps to determine the focus of instruction. Semantic Webbing is a strategy lesson for connecting and organizing ideas that teachers and students can use in various ways.

Who?

Students who need help in connecting and organizing ideas in meaning construction of text will benefit from this activity. Teachers and students can develop individual variations to apply in content areas.

How?

As a pre-reading or pre-writing activity introduce the strategy lesson in the following way:

1. Write a general topic or term on the chalkboard or overhead transparency. An example in the area of science is "space exploration."
2. Students suggest any related ideas that they associate with the topic; for example, space ships, astronauts, defense, galaxies, government, and so on. Write out the ideas suggested by the students.
3. Various suggestions are connected or organized by drawing lines to represent similar categories.
4. Students read the text to refine their webbing examples, or to expand some area of the subject for further reading or writing.

Then What?

1. The basic webbing of ideas can be rearranged as the reading and writing progresses. Exploration and expansion of ideas can lead to areas of interest for individual projects.
2. Different categories emerge, depending on the content area. A particular piece of literature can be webbed according to cause and effect, comparison and contrast, events, characters, settings, and so on.
3. Semantic webbing is used in reading and writing processes to clarify relationships and to coordinate ideas. It is also used as a post-reading or writing activity to organize factual recall of information by relating general-to-specific concepts.

Charting Information

By A. Geary

Why?

This activity helps readers focus on reading strategies and attitudes, and to develop metacognitive awareness. It gives students practice in organizing information, drawing conclusions, reading information on a chart, and reporting information in written form.

Who?

Students who need practice dealing with the organizational structure of informational text will benefit from this activity. When students are aware of their own reading attitudes and strategies, strategy instruction can be facilitated.

How?

1. Divide the students into groups with five to seven students in each group. Distribute three copies (see below) of the Burke Reading Interview (Modified for Older Readers). Students interview one of their group and a student outside the group. They take notes during the interview and, if possible, record it in order to fill in information later. Students organize the answers to each question into categories and display these on a chart.
2. Discuss how social scientists report the methodology and results of a survey in written form. Each student's written report should include at least three conclusions drawn from the data.
3. Talk about reading with the students. Discuss strategies that will help students move through the text and make sense of what they read. Discuss favorite books and share these with the entire group.

Burke Reading Interview (Modified for Older Readers)*

1. When you are reading and you come to something you don't know, what do you do?
   Do you ever do anything else?
2. Who is a good reader that you know?
3. What makes _____ a good reader?
4. Do you think _____ (the reader mentioned above) ever comes to something he or she doesn't know when reading?
5. When _____ comes to something he or she doesn't know, what do you think he or she does about it?
6. If you knew that someone was having difficulty reading, how would you help that person?
7. What would a teacher do to help that person?
8. How did you learn to read?
9. What would you like to do better as a reader?
10. Do you think that you are a good reader? Yes_____ No_____
11. What do you read routinely, like every day or every week?

12. What do you like most of all to read?
13. Can you remember any special book or the most memorable thing you have ever read?
14. What is the most difficult thing(s) you have to read?

Then What?

Other survey questions can be used, as well as other areas of study (such as sociology, economics, or psychology). Students can decide upon areas they wish to investigate and can develop, conduct, and report the results of their own surveys.

*"Burke Reading Interview" adapted from C. Burke by D. Watson, R. Robinson, E. Chippendale, *et al.*

The Advance Organizer and Essay Questions

By K. Sayler

Why?

Many students approach an essay test or paper with fear and frustration. Even though they can discuss the subject, when they begin to write they become unsure. How many facts should be mentioned? How many examples should be used to emphasize the argument? What should be included or omitted?

This strategy lesson gives students a structure for dealing with essay questions. It helps students to structure their thoughts before writing, and thus allows for earlier successes on essay papers and tests. As students become more adept at organizing their thoughts, the cues are eliminated.

Who?

This strategy lesson is useful with high-school students in classes that stress essay responses—English, social studies, and science.

How?

1. Select a number of questions from your subject area that require students to analyze material studied and show relationships to some common idea or theme. For example, in American history a question might be: "What was the destiny of the American Indian?" In English it might be: "How are Romeo and Juliet like people you know?"
2. Demonstrate and discuss with students how to make an advance organizer (Semantic Webbing [see Strategy 5.1], graphic cue system, chart, or outline) that contains the appropriate concepts and number of examples.
3. Students respond to the organizer before constructing an essay response, and construct pertinent information on the organizer itself.

Example

American Indians—Their Destiny
The American Indians' destiny was shaped by the attitudes of many groups: the government and the laws that were passed, the Indians' attitudes toward whites and the white people's attitudes toward American Indians, and the reactions of all three to the new homeland (reservation) given to the Indian.

In an essay explain the actions and attitudes of all three groups. Which was most important in shaping the destiny of the American Indian and why?

Advance organizer stemming from the question:

4. Using an overhead projector, discuss with students how each part of the organizer can become a point in the essay. Write the sample essay with them, using the information from the organizer. Relate information from the organizer to the various requirements of the essay question.
5. As the year goes on the organizers become less structured and detailed. Encourage students to make their own organizers as a rehearsal before answering essay questions. They may choose to use a web, graph, chart, or outline to help organize their thoughts.

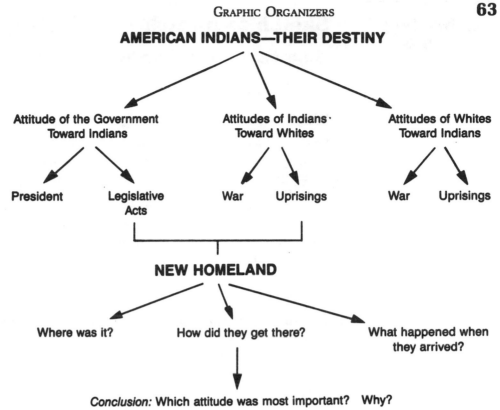

FIGURE 5.1 Example: American Indians—Their Destiny

Then What?

1. Students make organizers to review concepts. They trade the organizers and respond to their partners' questions.
2. Organizers can be used as "skinny books" (see Strategy 4.2) for students from later classes, who can build concepts before they begin the unit.

   Sample organizers follow:

   The question "What was the destiny of the American Indian?" is addressed in less structured organizers that can be used when students are constructing their own organizers or beginning to be more successful with essays. Eventually, students construct their own organizers from the essay questions themselves.

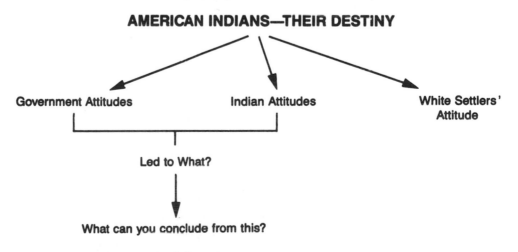

FIGURE 5.2 Less Structured Organizer

Sketch to Stretch

Adapted from J. Harste, C. Burke, and M. Siegel

Why?

Language users relate what they read to their backgrounds and experiences. Moving to another communication system, such as art, can assist learners in generating new insights and meanings. They may discover something about their responses to the text, its overall structure, interrelationships among characters, and so on. Since language users are engaged in a personal relationship with the text they are reading, it is likely that the sketches generated by this strategy lesson will vary among readers, contributing to the community experience with the text.

Who?

This strategy lesson is for all language users, especially for those who focus on isolated parts of a text—such as individual words—rather than the overall meaning and structure of the text.

How?

1. Find a book or story with a fairly explicit structure and form. Students read (or read aloud) the piece. After all readers have had a chance to complete the passage, it is put away.
2. Students draw what the story means, using one sheet of paper for their sketches. Students then share and discuss their sketches.

Then What?

1. Put all the sketches in a booklet with a copy of the story at the end. Students can examine all the sketches and then read the story with new insight.
2. As students complete self-selected books, they can generate sketches and put them on a bulletin board. These sketches serve as "advertisements" for particular books.
3. Sketch to Stretch can be used with content area texts.

Schema Stories

Adapted from D. Watson

Why?

Students learn story structures by listening to and reading literature. One way of continuing to develop a sense of story for various types of literature is to reconstruct and compare their organizational structures or schemas.

Who?

Students who need to further develop a sense of story or who have difficulty predicting what will happen in stories will profit from this strategy lesson.

How?

1. Select a narrative that has an easily identifiable beginning, clear plot development, and a definite ending. The story can be from a content area (social studies or science, for example) or other narrative.
2. Cut the story into sections (three to six sections are usually appropriate). Each section must be long enough to give readers something substantial to read—even though they might be reading something from the middle of the selection. It is important to choose a text that contains clear cohesive devices that connect the sections of the text; for example: "Once upon a time . . .," "secondly," "*That made him mad*," and so on.
3. Divide students into small groups. Each student in the group reads the selection silently, considering what might have happened before and after that excerpt. Students discuss their excerpt in the small groups.
4. Ask students to predict who might have the beginning of the story. The students who believe that they have the beginning read that section aloud. The others decide whether or not they agree that this is the first part. If they agree, the second section is called for, and the activity continues in this way with the remaining sections of the story.
5. More than one group may think that they have a particular section of the story. Call for the next section to resolve disagreements about the previous one. This type of discussion is what gives value to the strategy lesson because students are paying careful attention to story structure.
6. The entire text is read and the cohesive devices are identified and discussed.

Then What?

1. In social studies or science this activity can be used with the summary statement of the chapter as a review.
2. A single student can complete this activity.
3. Students can write their own selections to be used by the whole group.
4. Students in the group can put all of the sections in order except the ending, and then each one can write their own endings. These are read and discussed.

Possible resources:

Old textbooks
Magazines
Recipes
Brochures
Directions for games
Newspaper articles

<table>
<tr><td>☐ **Strategy** ☐
5.6</td></tr>
</table>

You're the Editor

By M. Bixby

Why?

Students should use whatever schema (categorization systems) they have developed to predict the organizing structures of texts they read. Novels and short stories have their own predictable structures, or "story grammars." By using the structure of a content area book's table of contents, readers can envision an overview of the chapter that is more helpful as a preview than the introduction to the chapter.

Who?

Students who read content area books and encounter difficulty with comprehension due to lack of background experience will benefit from this pre-reading activity.

How?

1. Working alone, in pairs, or in small groups, students pick chapters to be read.
2. Tell the students: "You're the editor." Discuss the role of textbook editors and the purpose of chapter introductions. Questions to address should include: "Why are there introductions to textbook chapters?" "What makes an introduction helpful?" "What would a reader need to know before reading a chapter?"
3. After the discussion students take the role of editors. They are to write introductions for the chapters they have picked, using only the information from the table of contents and their own background information. Good advice to use is that the introduction should help readers get ready to read the chapter.

Then What?

1. Students exchange and read one another's introductions and compare them to those in the text.
2. Discuss how helpful the student-written introductions are, as compared to the printed versions.
3. It is important for students to know that they can write introductions to chapters even if they do not know very much about the subject. By working together and brainstorming, students can "know" more about textbook chapters than they think they do.
4. These introductions are written to help students to establish schema prior to reading, so the writing need not be edited for classroom publication.
5. Students then read and discuss the chapters for which they have prepared.

6

Content Area Strategy Lessons

Every teacher is a teacher of language. This involves more than teaching *about* language: It means teachers engage students in authentic situations and explore content as they listen and read, and express content as they write and talk. Students use language to learn and to share what they know.

Teachers can help students become flexible readers by developing strategies for handling class texts. There is diversity in texts in terms of organizational structure and "friendliness"; that is, how well they match readers' experiences and background knowledge.

Teachers can help students learn through writing by providing opportunities for them to write to learn: to respond to what they read and hear, to take a variety of perspectives and points of view, and to write for a variety of audiences and purposes.

Teachers can help students become active oral language users. In addition to listening to the teacher talk, students talk and listen to each other in pairs, small groups, and large groups; discussion involves all learners.

The strategy lessons in this section embed the language processes in specific content areas—the fine arts, social studies, science, industrial arts, and math. These areas are not mutually exclusive; the following strategy lessons lend themselves to the integration of content. In addition, the general strategy lessons in the previous chapter are appropriate in content areas.

□ Strategy □ 6.1

Learning Logs
By F. Reynolds

Why?

Monitoring one's own learning process and progress (metacognition) is an important cognitive skill. The Learning Log used in classes to record and monitor process and progress helps students direct their learning and studying. It is also another way to promote fluency and flexibility in writing and shows how writing clarifies thinking.

Who?

All students need to develop metacognitive awareness and need practice in writing to learn.

How?

1. Direct students to re-examine the class by keeping a daily log in which they are to record first what occurred in class for the day. To help focus the lesson ask questions such as:

   "What did I learn today?"
   "What puzzled or confused me?"
   "What would help to clarify things for me?"
   "What did I enjoy, hate, accomplish in class today?"
   "How did I learn from the discussion or lesson?"
   "How was my performance in class?"

2. Students write for at least ten minutes each day. It would be helpful if the last five or ten minutes of each class period were devoted to the learning log.

3. Use the logs to see what content or processes need to be reviewed, clarified, or expanded. Write directly to students in the log entries.

Then What?

1. The logs could be the basis for teacher-student conferences.
2. Students who are computer competent could write their logs on a disc and make a printout when logs are due.

Activating Previous Knowledge

By F. Reynolds

Why?

One of the basic keys to good comprehension is connecting what a person already knows or has experienced with new material. This connecting enables students to predict outcomes, ask questions, synthesize, analyze, and evaluate. Thus, the activating of this previous knowledge is an important part of any strategy lesson.

Who?

All students need strategies for activating previous knowledge.

How?

Students may engage in:

1. Brainstorming or listing in which they write down all they already know.
2. Semantic webbing (see Strategy 5.1), where they use a topic or a key idea for the center and expand ideas.
3. Partner discussion, where they talk with partners or groups about what they already know or have experienced about a topic.
4. Using pictures or other visual aids to activate previous knowledge through writing or discussion.

Then What?

Any of these activities can be worked into any lesson plan as a pre-reading or pre-writing activity.

Perspective Research Guide

By R. Thompson

Why?

Students develop a personal perspective on issues by incorporating their own background information on the topic with new information gained through research. This content area strategy helps students become aware of their responsibilities in the learning process, and offers an open-ended structure that encourages students to make decisions and become "experts" in some area. By integrating related concepts from their pooled backgrounds and the new research they initiate, they develop a point of view through active research procedures.

Who?

This strategy lesson is valuable in any content area that stresses research, especially with students who tend to be teacher-dependent.

How?

1. Introduce a topic to be discussed. The topic can be chosen by you or the students. It should be general in nature, such as pollution, the West, and so on. Ask students what they already know about the subject and write these brainstormed ideas on the board.
2. Students write what they know about the subject. They can use the ideas on the board, expand on one idea, or write something which hasn't been mentioned. This is called "What I Know."
3. Students read articles from a variety of sources related to the subject. After reading the articles, students respond to the information either by taking notes or by discussing and writing their reactions to the material. Students label this "What I Found Out."
4. Students form small groups of three to five students and share the information and their reactions. They can go back to the information, maps, charts, and so on to verify what they are discussing. This discussion moves students into further research.
5. After the small group discussion each student ponders the information and writes an individual reaction called "This Makes Sense to Me." This step is the bringing together of the students' background information with the newly acquired information.

Then What?

After the writing time students return to whole group discussion where ideas of interest are listed under "How I Can Use This Information." Ideas may be the basis for further individual or small group research writing on the same subject, letters of inquiry, personal interviews, or other topics on which students may wish to do research.

Teacher Role-Playing

By R. Steffes and G. Grupe

Why?

Students and teachers enjoy a change of pace in the classroom. When formats, pace, and activities vary, everyone remains interested and challenged. By selecting appropriate scenes from literature or history, teachers can introduce units in new, exciting ways, as well as foster an appreciation for literature.

Who?

This strategy lesson can be used in any content area.

How?

1. Look through fiction (particularly historical fiction), plays, songs, and poems to be excerpted for a role-playing situation in your content area.
2. Enlist the help of a student (without the rest of the class knowing it), another teacher, an administrator, or a parent to set up the role-playing situation. Since the element of surprise is crucial, vary the players.
3. Find costumes, such as a robe or items to carry, that will help create a mood.
4. Use the scenes to introduce a unit, summarize a unit, or present a new problem within a unit.
5. The following two examples show how role-playing can create excitement and interest in an American Studies class (using a teacher and a student) and an English class (using two teachers).

Scene: An American Studies Classroom

As students settle into their seats, the tardy bell rings and the teacher walks in dressed in a powdered wig and black flowing robe. He looks around the room quickly (as a few giggles begin to surface) and wickedly points a finger at a young girl sitting near a bank of windows.

"There she sits among us, a heretic, a blasphemer who dares to interpret the Bible herself!" the teacher shouts at the girl.

The girl bravely leaps from her chair and in a furious tone retorts, "Who has given you the right to criticize me? The Bible is for everyone to read and interpret within themselves. I do not need to be told how to worship God! The Lord has revealed himself to me!"

For a few minutes, the teacher and student continue, both moving toward each other, their tempers beginning to peak, and the seventeenth-century story of Anne Hutchinson comes to life.

Scene: An English Classroom

Across the hall two English teachers walk into the room. One is dressed rather shabbily, wearing black gloves and carrying a large black tin box. He is cast as an attorney. The other is dressed impeccably from head to toe, and walks with a great deal of confidence.

Sensory Images

By E. Dean

Why?

Imagery appeals to the senses and comes alive in the personal communication between the language user and the text. The richness of a particular book depends on this relationship.

Who?

Readers who restrict themselves to literal interpretations of text or who believe that all meaning is supplied by the author will benefit from this activity.

How?

1. Select a variety of materials that appeal to the senses and discuss the imagery in each. Materials can include:
   Descriptive historical fiction about an important event.
   A picture or drawing depicting soldiers knee-deep in mud in a jungle.
   Poetry that appeals to the senses.
2. Students make a chart with each of the senses at the top of the columns:

Sight	Hearing	Taste	Smell	Touch

   For each of the materials chosen, brainstorm language to describe the scene and write these descriptions in the appropriate columns.
3. Using the descriptions in the columns, the students write about how they would feel in those situations.

Then What?

1. Students can illustrate or write a script for a particular scene.
2. Choose one of the senses and write an original piece that emphasizes that sense, for instance, the noise of the fans at a basketball game or the smells in the forest after a rainstorm.
3. Read a student authored and a professionally authored piece and select specific scenes that involve the senses. Discuss and write about the descriptions used in these scenes.
4. Clip newspaper articles using sensory images for a collage for the bulletin board. This can be accompanied by a written commentary of the sensory images.

Picture Tunes

By S. R. Crenshaw

Why?

This activity encourages students to become involved in literacy by sharing their understanding of and interest in current popular music.

Who?

The activity is applicable to many students but is particularly designed to assist the reluctant readers and writers in understanding the possibilities of meaningful communication through various modes.

How?

1. Students name or make a list of the top ten musical selections. Initiate a general discussion of particular favorites and reasons for those choices. The class can vote and make a general list of their top choices.
2. Partners work together on a particular song, writing the words to the music from memory. Groups assist one another when lyrics are incomplete. Suggest that they bring in printed or typed copies for the next class session.
3. Discuss the meanings of particular songs. Are there social or political connections? What about controversial or objectionable themes? Is there a problem with censorship? Ask students to suggest alternative lyrics to alleviate objectionable material. Are the lyrics acceptable for illustration? How would students design illustrations to convey meanings?
4. Sketch ideas for alternatives to commercially produced music videos. Focus on the theme of the song, and connect the visual with the meaning as interpreted by students.

Then What?

1. Do research on the top tunes for various years in the past. Compare and contrast the themes, use of vocabulary, and meanings suggested with current popular works. Discuss the differences in picturing tunes of the past.
2. Partners can select a particular song, type or print phrases or portions of lyrics on separate sheets of paper, and draw or select pictures that illustrate the essence of the song. The collected works may be bound together for an illustrated songbook.

Textual Art

By S. R. Crenshaw

Why?

The aesthetic experience is varied for individuals depending on context, experience, and interest. The awareness that perceptions differ is an important concept that may be applied to varying situations.

Who?

This strategy lesson is for students who need to develop an appreciation for art in general and for others' opinions in particular.

How?

1. Select five or six slides or prints of works of art. Present one at a time to the class or to individuals. Without giving any background, ask students to react in writing to one or more of the pictures without talking to anyone.
2. Guided questions can facilitate the writing process:

   Does this remind you of something in your experience?
   How does this make you feel?
   What is the most interesting feature you noticed?
   Is there a predominant color or shape you like?
3. Students indicate their choices to someone else and talk about them.
4. After a sharing period the class discusses some of their reactions with the whole group.

   Were there similarities in descriptive terms and choices?
   Were there problems in putting feelings into words?
   What kinds of words were used most frequently?

   Talk about the process of translating visual forms to written forms. Emphasize the variety of responses to the same material and discuss the reasons for the differences.
5. Collect reading materials that provide information about the artist and his or her work. Ask students to do their own research on particular artists, and share with the class.
6. After a period of information-gathering, display the art prints or slides again and ask for written reactions. Discuss the experience of translating art into text, and the differing perceptions of individuals.

Then What?

1. A classroom art gallery can be developed with contributions by students using various art forms (sculpture, painting, drawing, and so on).
2. Student art projects on paper can be bound into a class book with descriptions of the works and the artists' profiles.

Sketch and Stretch Mythology*

Adapted from J. Harste, C. Burke, and M. Siegel

Why?

This activity helps readers focus on the meaning and structure of text, and relate these meanings through alternative forms of communication.

Who?

This is beneficial for students who need alternative forms of expressing concepts.

How?

1. Find out what students know about mythology, and discuss the myths they remember. Read Greek, Roman, Norse, Hopi, Navajo, and other myths to the students.
2. Students illustrate a character, creature, scene, or theme from the myth. Sketches can be transferred to poster board and enhanced with color. Individuals or groups present their projects to the class and give a synopsis of the plot.

Then What?

1. Students can adapt this activity to other literary forms.
2. You can read the myths aloud while students sketch their ideas as the plot progresses.

*See "Sketch to Stretch," Strategy 5.4.

<table>
<tr><td>☐ Strategy ☐
6.10</td></tr>
</table>

Theme Units
By F. Reynolds

Why?

Theme units in any content area class—English, social studies, science, and so on—are a very natural way to integrate all of the language arts (reading, writing, listening, speaking, and thinking) and to teach a concept or concepts. Goals and objectives for a unit are set based on the needs, interests, and experiences of students. Materials can then be collected from a variety of sources, and activities can be planned. Usually, enthusiasm is high in a theme unit because students feel they have control over what and how they learn.

Who?

All students benefit from making choices about the subjects they explore.

How?

1. Students and teachers decide which concepts/ideas/content need to be taught, and write goals and objectives.
2. Gather materials using all sources and resources; i.e., school library and librarian, magazines, newspapers, community resources, other teachers and students, parents, old texts, current texts, and so on. Criteria for choosing materials include a variety and choice of current and interesting reading materials at several reading levels. Add pictures, charts, and graphs for more information and interest.

Then What?

Plan language arts activities around the content:

Writing—expressive, poetic and social kinds of writing activities (journals, logs, notes, directions, letters, responses, essays and essay tests, and so on).

Reading—print materials from all sources for all levels.

Listening—to each other in pairs, small groups, and whole class; to the teacher; to guest speakers; to audiovisual materials.

Speaking—in small and large groups, oral reports, discussions, oral quizzes, etc.

Thinking—all activities and materials need to be designed to elicit critical and creative thinking, not just linear thinking.

The March of Progress

By J. Henson

Why?

This activity enables students to see history as a progression of changes over time that affect both people and their environment, and to express these changes through writing and art. This activity gives students a visual reminder of what they have studied.

Who?

Secondary history students will benefit from this activity.

How?

1. Divide students into three groups; these groups can change during the year. As each unit is completed, one group summarizes the important events, dates, and personalities in writing. The second group depicts the summary information in a mural. The mural should include representative flora, fauna, and persona; this is called a "World" mural. The third group does research on the history of their town or city, and depicts the area as it might have looked at that particular point in history. This is an "Our Town" mural.
2. As the year progresses, subsequent written summaries and World and Our Town murals emerge, and are displayed in the classroom. Events could include Boston, 1776; San Juan, 1890; Pearl Harbor, 1941; My Lai, Vietnam, 1965; and so on. Corresponding Our Town murals could be designed for past years such as 1776, 1890, 1941, 1965, and so on.

Then What?

1. A variety of writings can emerge from such an activity, including comparisons and contrasts of Our Town and the places being studied, the ecological impacts of historical events, and the written history of Our Town.
2. Display the murals around the school.
3. Invite people from the community to share their memories. These memories can be depicted in the murals.

History Book

By L. H. Trickey

Why?

The study of history can seem irrelevant to students if they do not see how it influences them. Many students are not aware of significant historical events that take place in their own communities. This activity is designed to make history more personal by having students visit sites of historical interest that are close to their homes. It is interdisciplinary in nature and involves doing research, reading critically, taking photographs or making drawings, writing, and reporting.

Who?

This activity is for secondary social studies students.

How?

1. Talk with students about possible places in their community that have historical importance. Brainstorm a list of such places and write these on the board. Students decide if they wish to visit the community sites individually or in groups.
2. Work together to bring information about these sites into the classroom. Pamphlets, brochures, newspapers, and information from the Chamber of Commerce and library are possible sources.
3. Students pick three sites and do research on them to help them get ready for the visits. They may use the school, public library, or community resource people to help them do the research on chosen sites.
4. Students, individually or as groups, visit their sites, taking photographs and making drawings. The subjects of the drawings and photos are up to the students, but they should include the most significant characteristic of the site.
5. Using the photographs and drawings and the information found during research, students prepare a "history book" on the sites they have visited. They can also add an "Author's Commentary." Here the students express their own thoughts on the significance of the sites, including their overall significance in American history.

Then What?

1. Students can present the information so that all members of the class can hear it.
2. Students can share their books with one another.
3. Although this activity is used in social studies it also lends itself to other content areas, such as earth science (visiting rock formations, creeks, and streams nearby) or biology (finding examples of flora and fauna).

You Are There
By K. Clapp

Why?

This activity moves the reader into the "picture" regarding historical events, their causes and their repercussions.

Who?

Students in history classes are helped to discover relationships among past, present, and future.

How?

1. Students form study groups of three or four and read about a particular era or event in their texts.
2. Each student assumes the role of a character, representing a particular group involved in the event being studied (for example: clergy, politician, aristocrat, peasant, soldier). Students imagine that their characters are their ancestors.
3. Students write about their identities to bring out feelings, attitudes, and values.

Then What?

1. Students can write a play and act it out for other classes.
2. They can trace their assumed "ancestors" from the time being studied to the present on a family tree or time line.
3. Students can write a letter from their character to descendants about the historical event and their part in it.

Diary of an Immigrant

By M. Henrichs

Why?

Diary writing sharpens personal expression. This activity attempts to capture the feelings of new Americans who traditionally have changed the face of the nation.

Who?

This activity can be used with social studies classes at the secondary level.

How?

1. Students read a *Time* magazine aricle such as "Immigrant," July 8, 1985. Develop a list of available reading materials that deal with the topic of immigration present and past.
2. Students think about what it might have been like to emigrate to a new country, not knowing the language and with few job skills. Try to capture both the excitement and the problems that the immigrants faced in leaving their homeland, the voyage, and their arrival in America. List students' ideas on the board.
3. Students take the role of a modern-day immigrant or one from another period in American history. Students might like to emigrate from a country of their ancestors.
4. Students keep a diary on how they imagine the thoughts, feelings, and experiences of immigrants preparing for and encountering life in a new country. The entries should extend over a period of time. They may begin just before departure and include the voyage and the first few weeks in America.

Then What?

1. Small group sessions can focus on the contributions made and the problems faced by immigrants from specific countries.
2. Large group discussions can center on immigration in its historical perspective: the problems, contributions, and social integration of immigrants past and present.

Mission Impossible

By L. Byrne

Why?

When learners are involved with the material being studied, learning is enhanced. By exploring history as a personal journey students can appreciate that *real* stories can be told about distant events and people, bringing them into focus.

Who?

This activity is appropriate for students studying geography or history. The example used here is for students studying Europe during World War II.

How?

1. Students read a variety of texts about World War II, along with discussions, films, and lectures about the topic.
2. Divide the class into small groups. Each group acts as a spy team and is given a mission. The mission is written or recorded in the style of the "Mission Impossible" television program. For example, a mission can read: "You are a group of Allied spies who have been dropped behind enemy lines in Germany. You must go to Munich and Berlin to collect information about those cities and surrounding communities for an Allied invasion. Your mission, should you decide to accept it, is to study the areas and gather all available information that would help the Allies: a map, weather conditions, industry in the area, and any other valuable information you identify. You are then to report back to a special task force in London for debriefing. You will need to establish the shortest and safest route for your return to London."
3. Students divide the tasks of gathering information for their missions from available texts, maps, the Weather Service, and any other appropriate and available sources. They are responsible for coordinating the information and reporting back to their superiors in London.
4. Divide the class into groups to represent the different theaters of action during World War II—Europe, Africa, and the Pacific.

Then What?

This activity can be integrated with other content areas such as science and math.

International Invention Convention

By G. Grupe and R. Steffes

Why?

When concepts are linked to a personal experience, learning becomes easier and students remember more. This activity gives students the simulated experience of being an inventor. It brings together experiences from math, drama, art, English, economics, and history, producing an integrated project.

Who?

All students benefit from seeing the interrelatedness of school curricula.

How?

1. Discuss what a patent is, how it is granted, and its use. Tell students that they have an opportunity to become inventors. First, they need to think of an invention. It must be original, workable, and logical. They apply for their patent from the teacher. Use a form from the Patent Office to make a replica. Students include drawings of the invention, possible uses, materials that are needed, and purchase price.

2. Upon attaining the patent, students begin a marketing strategy that involves:

   Writing a news article about the product.
   Writing a detailed description of the product for possible financial backers.
   Creating advertisements for radio or TV to sell the product.
   Preparing financial budgets and projections.
   Making a poster or working model for displays and sales presentations.

3. Following marketing activities, inventors are invited to the International Invention Convention. (The classroom becomes a convention complete with balloons, streamers, and refreshments.) Students display their products and solicit other students to be investors and potential buyers.

4. Inventors are invited to present a one- to five-minute presentation/demonstration in order to educate other conventioneers of the value and usefulness of the product.

Then What?

At the end of the convention students have first-hand experience with the process inventors go through. The class discusses and shares insights gained from the activity.

□ Strategy □
6.17

Civil Rights Writes

By C. Gilles, J. Henson, and G. Grupe

Why?

Using literature to illustrate concepts can lead to a better understanding of these concepts as well as to a heightened appreciation for literature. Asking students to read and question one another in written conversations (see Strategy 4.4) gets students to "write on the edge of what they know" (Calkins, 1985). Their conversations can be far more thought-provoking than a teacher-led discussion. This can, in turn, lead to more reading and writing.

Who?

Secondary students studying the civil rights movement will benefit from reading and writing to learn.

How?

1. Students choose partners and each reads either Martin Luther King's "I Have a Dream" speech or an excerpt from Dick Gregory's *Nigger*. Students read these pieces silently, and consider these questions while reading:

    How would you feel if you were Martin Luther King?
    What does reading about the civil rights movement remind you of?
2. After reading, students write down one question and pass it to their partners. Students use these questions to begin a written conversation.
3. Circulate around the room and enter into the conversations. After the writing is completed, discuss the pieces, using the written conversations as a departure point for further study.

Then What?

1. Students can view film clips of Martin Luther King's marches and react in writing.
2. Some students may do research on the passive resistance movements of Gandhi and Martin Luther King, and share the information with the class. They can also see the movie *Gandhi*.

Making Connections in Content Classes

By C. Gilles

Why?

Students learn and remember when they link new information to familiar concepts and events. Some students have difficulty making connections between abstract concepts and real examples. Using the newspaper and novels to illustrate concepts of American government makes content more concrete, and also provides opportunities for students to improve their reading and writing abilities. It allows for individuality and student choices.

Who?

Students who have difficulty understanding abstract concepts and students who see little connection between school and their out-of-school experiences will benefit from this activity.

How?

1. In order to provide a wide range of materials to illustrate textbook concepts, collect passages from a variety of sources to illustrate concepts. List the bibliographic information or photocopy the passages and keep them in a large notebook or file. They can be used when members of the class need them. Encourage students to add passages they have found in their reading.
2. The "notebook notes" offer additional choices to students. For example, if a student has difficulty with a particular text the notes provide an alternative passage. The passages can be used to build a conceptual background for students who are not yet ready to read the target text (see "Skinny Books," Strategy 4.2), or used as a resource for reports or presentations.
3. Help students "make connections" by:

   Keeping a Learning Log (see Strategy 6.1), where they react and respond to the passages.
   Collecting newspaper articles that illustrate concepts.
   Presenting the article or passage to the class as an illustrative example of a particular concept.
   Role-playing situations in which the concept can occur in their lives.

   Students can also make connections by discussing the articles and how they exemplify the concepts. Encourage students to attend real events that relate to what they are learning.

   #### Example
   The following is an example of merging the study of the Bill of Rights with a novel and a newspaper:
   When studying different governments the class considers the rights of people in democracies and considers what rights people in some non-democratic governments are denied.
   Students are encouraged to use the daily newspaper to research articles that illustrate democracy and the rights of people under other systems of government. They are encouraged to study areas in detail, to become "experts."

In one class students found apartheid in South Africa an important issue to consider. Students volunteered to follow the issue of apartheid and reported back to the entire class. Others became interested in finding out more about apartheid and wrote letters to a local information clearinghouse.

The class invited a guest speaker to talk about South Africa. As students learned various things about the country each student became a resource in the classroom. One discovered that there was going to be a peaceful demonstration regarding apartheid at a local university. The class attended, and saw the "right of assembly" occurring before their eyes. They heard speakers compare the plight of black South Africans to that of Black Americans; and they began to understand how the concepts being studied impacted on peoples' lives.

In addition to the newspaper, novels such as *Animal Farm* by George Orwell can provide striking examples of topics of study, in this case, the study of government. Students read each chapter in the book and then record their thoughts in a "learning log" (see Strategy 6.1) in which they write both what is happening in the book and their personal reactions. Concepts like "oppression," "dictatorship," and "constitution" take on strong meanings when coming alive in the context of the characters and their lives at Manor Farm.

Then What?

In the class described above the issue of rights guaranteed to citizens permeated the entire year. Students remained interested in apartheid and *Animal Farm* and have chosen to follow the issues on their own outside of class. When students are given wide parameters, encouraged to "make connections" between themselves and their learning, and become experts in some area, they accept more responsibility for their own learning and become life-long learners.

Science and Practical Arts

<table>
<tr><td>□ Strategy □
6.19</td><td><h2>Science—Picture and Reading Stations</h2>By F. Reynolds, from ideas by I. Pickett</td></tr>
</table>

Why?

In the science classroom lab stations are very much a part of the regular activities. These lab stations provide "hands-on" experiences with plants, animals, chemicals, physical properties, and so on; and help students to visualize the concepts they are learning about. Using pictures and text from a variety of books at "stations" not only varies the usual classroom routine of "reading the chapter and answering the questions at the end" but also provides active learning—meaning involvement with and, therefore, more in-depth comprehension of concepts. An important thing to remember when setting up stations is to combine visual, writing, and reading experiences.

Who?

Secondary science students benefit from "hands-on" experiences.

How?

1. Picture stations can be set up to help illustrate and give variety to any science situation. For example, in a unit on ecology, pictures of different biomes can be set up at different stations around the room, and the students then go to each station and identify the biome from a picture and describe it in writing and/or answer some questions about it. A textbook or other reading source should be handy for students to help them identify the pictures.
2. A reading station can be set up with excerpts from many sources on a certain concept. Students then go from station to station; read the excerpts; write their reactions, ideas, notes, and so on in their learning logs (see Strategy 6.1).

Then What?

Combine pictures and reading for another set of stations, or combine additional "friendly" texts with experiments.

Writing in Science—Explanation Pieces
By F. Reynolds, from ideas by I. Pickett

Why?

An "explanation" piece of writing is done when the student knows the answer to a problem and writes to explain a concept(s) logically. To help students become scientifically literate (meaning having basic knowledge in science "and using skills of communication in science—the ability to read, write, and express one's opinion on scientific matters," Guthrie, 1983, p. 286) writing-to-learn strategy lessons in conjunction with the content area reading, science labs, and audiovisual materials help students clarify concepts, review material, try out new ideas, and make connections to other material and to their lives.

Who?

Students in any area of science benefit from writing explanation pieces.

How?

The teacher and the class think of concepts that need to be clarified after being introduced. For example, in the area of genetics, after a discussion of genes and inheritance factors a short paper might be written on "How do two brown-eyed parents get a blue-eyed child?" Or, in a unit on ecology, after a discussion on water or air pollution, a short paper might be written on "How and why does diffusion occur in the water with certain pollutants?"

Short "explanation" papers can be used to help clarify any concepts taught that need further work by the students.

Then What?

1. If a student is particularly mystified by a concept then a piece could be written on what areas of the new learning are particularly obscure. After several of these explanation pieces the concept is often understood.
2. From "explanation" pieces students could write "expansion" pieces, which extend the concept to fit other situations.

Writing in Science—Reading Journal Variation

By F. Reynolds, from ideas by I. Pickett

Why?

Some people think that good literature belongs only in the English class and rarely think of good fiction and nonfiction in a science class. However, good literature can entertain and inform. Writings by Lewis Thomas, for example, entertain, inform, and provide "literary" experiences. The following strategy lesson gives students reading choices, alternative information sources, and a chance to write freely in journals.

Who?

Secondary school students in any area of science benefit from reading and writing about relevant literature.

How?

For quarter or semester projects:

1. Have a selection of your favorite books relating to science—any area of the physical or hard sciences, such as biography/autobiography, nature journals, essays, and so on. Share them with the class. Have a wider selection of books and possible reading lists available in the library and classroom. Librarians could also give a book talk on selections.
2. Students choose a book that appeals to them and read it. As they read the book they write eight to ten journal entries on their responses and reactions to the different chapters, pieces, concepts, or ideas. These entries are turned in at regular intervals for the teacher's response, and can also be shared in small groups.

For short projects:

1. Follow the guidelines above, except use magazine articles and write only one to three entries in a journal.
2. Students share as above, or write brief summary reviews and then share.

Then What?

1. Instead of nonfiction, use science fiction or outdoor/nature fiction.
2. Students watch television science programs and keep a viewer journal.

Life Science Riddles

By C. Gilles

Why?

Proficient writing often takes a backseat to "learning the content." Even though the act of writing helps students to learn, students are often required to spend their time on worksheets that require a minimum of writing and reading. This activity is a summation to a unit on "life in a pond." Students use information learned in life science to provide clues for a riddle.

Who?

Junior high school students studying ecosystems and pond life will benefit from writing and reading to learn.

How?

1. After studying the animal and plant life in and around ponds, students pick an organism they especially liked. Each student writes a riddle describing the plant or animal in the first person. Each line contains a new and more descriptive clue. Clues can be related to kingdom; phylum; how the animal looks, breathes, eats, moves, reproduces; what enemies the organism has; and how the organism benefits man.
2. Riddles are exchanged with partners and guessed at; or students can take turns reading them to the entire class and let the class guess.

Then What?

1. Riddles can be compiled into a book as a review of the unit or as an introduction to the unit for the following year (see Strategy 4.2).
2. Riddles can be used to review for a test on the unit.
3. To practice classification, students can group the riddles by various characteristics, such as how the organisms breathe, reproduce, eat, and so on.

Example of a life science riddle:

I am in the animal kingdom;
I am in the vertebrata phylum;
I am usually green, but I can be olive or black;
I breathe with lungs;
I eat frogs, toads, and insects;
I lay eggs, sometimes as many as 80;
I move very quickly; I am hard to catch;
King snakes and black snakes eat me;
I am helpful to man because I can eat gophers and young squirrels which might eat crops.
What am I?
(Garter snake)

□ Strategy □
6.23

Reading and Writing in the Shop

By F. Reynolds

Why?

Capitalizing on vocational interests through newspapers, tool catalogs, hobby/avocation magazines, and repair manuals and guides is a useful way to increase student interest in reading and writing.

Who?

Students in vocational classes will benefit from reading practical materials and making connections between them and school experiences. Students in applied language arts classes, too, will benefit from reading practical materials in their interest areas.

How?

1. Students write in journals before class: "What I need to do today is . . .," "How I will do it . . .," "Tools and procedures . . .," and so on. Or, write after class on what was accomplished and will happen the next day.
2. Students explain specific procedures or directions in learning logs (see Figure 6.1). Students write paragraphs using specific vocabulary to explain a procedure so that a novice would understand and be able to follow it.
3. Using the pictures in tool catalogues, repair manuals and guides, and hobby magazines like *Popular Mechanics* or *Popular Science*, students read to interpret, identify problems and solutions, and write a short narrative explaining the procedure or problem.
4. Students use tool catalogues for skimming activities. Give students problems to work on; *e.g.,* "You have a project to do that needs specific tools which you need to buy and only $ _____ to buy them with. Use the catalogue to find what you need." This is a good place to comparison shop on quality and price.
5. Have students read articles of interest to them on practical problems they may have, and give oral reports and/or demonstrations to the rest of the class.

Then What?

Students could do library and on-site, practical research on topics of interest to them, write reports, and give demonstrations and talks on these projects.

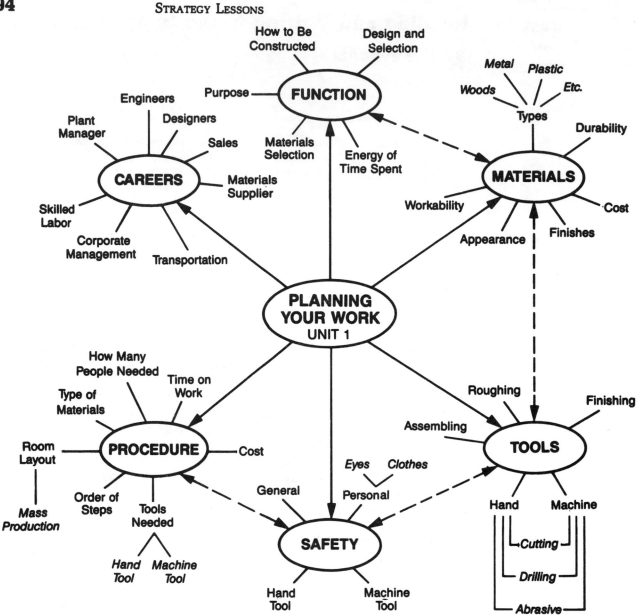

FIGURE 6.1 Graphic Organizer for "Planning Your Work"

Planning Your Work (Selecting, Designing, and Planning Projects)

By S. Wymore

Why?

This activity helps students in industrial arts classes to focus on prior knowledge related to planning projects and to build confidence.

Who?

Students in industrial arts classes who need to develop better insight regarding preparation, planning, and developing projects will benefit from this activity.

How?

1. Discuss what planning involves and why it is necessary. The students consider the class project to be completed, and generate a list of the steps they predict would be involved in the project. Discuss other projects related to the current one.
2. Students preview and read the text material. Students generate and share questions from the reading. These form the basis for general class discussion.
3. Students graphically organize information (diagram, webbing, outline, and so on; see Figure 6.1) and consider their original list of steps. This list is revised based on text information. The project plans are posted in the room and copies distributed to each student.

Then What?

1. "I remember . . . " (see Strategy 4.11) is used in the next class session to brainstorm the remembered information from the previous class. Provide the opportunity for re-reading the materials to clarify understanding.
2. Evaluation includes a self-evaluation form, along with the completion of the project.

□ Strategy □
6.25

The Math Story

By A. Corn

Why?

In order to solve problems students must read to find the connection between the information provided in the "story" and the mathematical question to be answered; and they must figure out a plan for answering the question. Often, practice problems in textbooks are unrelated to students' interests, purposes, and backgrounds. By writing their own math problems, students can more easily understand the relationship between concrete events and mathematical concepts.

Who?

All students can benefit from creating word problems that make mathematical concepts personally meaningful. The following suggestions deal mainly with fundamental concepts.

How?

1. Help students discover definitions for mathematical operations by providing objects that can be manipulated. Units of objects—boxes of paper clips, pencils, and the like—are readily available. Students can share their definitions through writing, diagramming, or demonstration. Once students develop familiarity with the "language" of math operations, help students find opportunities to use mathematics in order to solve problems.
2. Divide students into groups with five to seven members in a group. The group leader gives a number sentence, and group members write story problems. The group discusses the problems and determines ways of improving them.
3. Students can select a job from the classified ads and compute the hourly wage if the weekly rate is given, or the weekly rate if the yearly wage is given. Then they develop a budget based on their projected earnings.
4. They can study the sports pages in the newspaper. Compute the statistics for a favorite team or athlete.
5. They can choose a city they would like to visit and compute and compare the costs of driving, flying, or traveling there by bus.
6. They can write a mystery story that can be solved by identifying an unknown quantity (X).

Then What?

1. Individual conferences or group discussion of students' story problems can help you become aware of misunderstandings and areas of difficulty.
2. Individual folders of students' writings serve as valuable records of students' progress.
3. Students can make a book of word problem strategies.

<table>
<tr><td>☐ Strategy ☐
6.26</td></tr>
</table>

Writing in the Math Class

By E. Ahlbrandt, H. Holroyd, and F. Sharp

Why?

Writing in the math class will help teachers understand students' math backgrounds, attitudes, and anxieties. It will help students see their successes and understand their confusions.

Who?

Students in secondary level mathematics classes will benefit from writing about the studying, trying, and solving of math problems.

How?

Students and teachers write at least once a week. For student writing:

1. Describe how they prepared for a test:

   What problems were worked or reworked?
   How long did they study?
   What was memorized?
   Did they use class notes?

2. When tests are graded, students share their responses.
3. Students write the teacher notes about concepts they do not understand, or make up word problems or review sheets for other classes, or explain a mathematics problem or process by writing detailed explanations, or write to a student who was absent and explain the lesson.
4. Write to younger students telling what is expected of higher-level mathematics courses.
5. Keep a daily or weekly journal about how students learn mathematics (see Strategy 6.1).
6. Write about a homework problem they enjoyed or did not enjoy, and why.

Then What?

1. Type excerpts to share in class, and pick two or three excerpts to read aloud.
2. Write positive comments in the journals, or ask students to exchange papers for a sharing time.
3. Occasionally share your own writing with students.
4. Create a story or poem where a math problem is used.

Keep Them Thinking

By K. Deposki

Why?

Math is a challenge for many students, particularly when it involves abstract problems. Thinking puzzles that include inductive and deductive reasoning encourage students to think more logically. Students can build on these problem-solving exercises to organize solutions to mathematical problems.

Who?

This activity is helpful to those students who need opportunities to experience success in making observations, organizing ideas, and applying critical thinking.

How?

1. Initiate the activity by providing a number of logic puzzles for individual or small group participation. The students receive logic puzzles with questions to solve. They can work alone, with a partner, or in a small group.
2. Students list all the possible solutions that make sense and present their lists to the rest of the class. The suggestions are discussed and evaluated to determine the most likely answer for each puzzle.
3. If a reasonable solution is not evident, provide clues or hints to guide the problem-solving. After the answer has been revealed, the class reviews the process to determine what factors were involved in arriving at the correct solution.
4. This activity is then applied to math in the form of word problems.

Then What?

1. Students can find different logic puzzles to share with the class. A class period can be set aside to go through those puzzles.
2. Students can create their own logic and thinking puzzles.
3. Students apply the experience by identifying the types of thinking used to solve the puzzles, and making application to problem-solving in everyday situations both in and out of school.

Examples of Thinking Puzzles:
1. A man was in the middle of a large deep lake. He had no boat. He could not swim; and he could not float. No one else was around. He got to the shore safely all by himself. How did he do it?
2. Four people were together in a building at the ground level. When one person moved, they all moved. Why?
3. Two volumes of a book are standing side by side in order on a bookshelf. A bookworm begins eating at page one of volume one and eats its way straight through to the last page of volume two. If each cover is an eighth of an inch thick, and each book with the cover is two inches thick, how far does the bookworm travel?

CONTENT AREA STRATEGY LESSONS

Answers
1. The lake was frozen.
2. They used a revolving door.
3. One-fourth of an inch.

7

Strategy Lessons Using Newspapers and Other Sources

The newspaper has long been recognized as a valuable resource for current events and many content areas. Similarly, the use of trade books, magazines, pamphlets, catalogues, and other print materials extends school reading beyond textbooks. It is important that students use alternative print materials in the classroom, just as they use them naturally in their out-of-school lives.

This section focuses on the newspaper and includes ideas for using other resource materials in meaningful ways. The strategy lessons are invitations for teachers and students to sample from the rich world of print in the context of meaningful classroom experiences.

Share the News

By C. Gilles, M. Bixby, and P. Crowley

Why?

This activity provides meaningful reasons for reading the newspaper. It helps students gain experience in writing for a particular audience and solidify concepts by explaining them in writing to others with less background information. The activity also provides students with an opportunity to be "experts" on current events.

Who?

When readers have the opportunity to express in their own words through speaking or writing what they have read, comprehension is enhanced. When the author knows and considers the audience's background experiences and knowledge, the text is easier to comprehend. This activity will benefit upper-level students by giving them a chance to express what they know, and younger students who read what older students write.

How?

1. Students bring newspaper articles of interest to class. News about the community, state, or nation is preferable to features.
2. Discuss the stories and the difficulties they may present to someone unfamiliar with particular concepts. Students work with partners and rewrite the articles for younger students who may have difficulty reading the original pieces. Remind the authors that they must consider their audience and use concepts and labels that are familiar to younger students. Pictures, diagrams, and charts are valuable additions.
3. Partners revise and edit the pieces. Final forms can be typed as a "news magazine" and duplicated to distribute to younger students.

Then What?

1. Younger students read the articles and send their reactions and questions back to the older students.
2. Younger students can write a "news magazine" for older students. Their school news would be a source of topics.
3. Older students can extend this communication by presenting plays or skits to younger students.

Problem-Solving with the Newspaper

By P. Crowley

Why?

The newspaper is a valuable tool for developing concepts from a variety of content areas in a relevant, timely way. Many students do not read the "news" section of the newspaper, however, because they feel the content is not related to them. When students are asked to read the news, they often read it just to get facts. This strategy lesson helps students form and refine their attitudes, opinions, and understanding of what they read.

Who?

Students who need to be aware that there is more than one point of view on an issue and need experience in evaluating and forming opinions on an issue will benefit from this activity.

How?

1. Students read different news articles on a local, national, or international issue of their choice. After reading the articles, students write about the problems stated in the article along with the solutions offered (if any).
2. Students consider the problems and generate a list of their own solutions. When they cannot think of any more solutions, they break into groups and pass their papers around the group, and have their classmates add as many other solutions as they can think of.
3. When the papers are returned, students pick the solution they like best from the list (it can be their solution or someone else's, including the author's), write a more complete analysis of the problem, and defend the feasibility of the solution.

Then What?

1. Students can suggest a problem they see in their school, community, or beyond, and present this problem to their peers following the same procedure described above.
2. The opinions in "Letters to the Editor" columns or editorials from the newspaper can be used.
3. Students can write letters to local newspapers stating their opinions on an issue.
4. A school or class newspaper gives students an opportunity to take an active part in investigating problems and their solutions.

Extending the Newspaper

By A. Travers

Why?

Writing and publishing a classroom newsletter allows students to work together and encourages reading, writing, and thinking. It utilizes the students' experiences and backgrounds in a purposeful reading and writing activity, and gives students the opportunity to write for an audience.

Who?

This activity is beneficial to all students by helping them see themselves as authors writing for publication.

How?

1. Bring various newspapers to class and discuss the different sections in order to help students decide what they would like in their newsletter.
2. Determine with students the format for the newsletter and when it is to be published. If the class wants the newsletter to be published frequently, the format must be kept fairly simple.
3. Students choose the section of the newsletter they want to work on. Possible choices are:

   classroom news
   comics
   feature stories
   editorials
   horoscopes
   classified ads/display ads
   sports
   advice column

4. After the articles have been written, editors read and revise news stories and lay out the newsletter. Students serve as editors for one another; outside volunteers, such as parents, can also be involved.
5. Students publish the newsletter and share it with a number of audiences, including their families and others in the school.

Then What?

1. Students can write letters to the editor of the local newspaper in response to current events.
2. News can be gathered from the rest of the school and/or community for the newsletter.
3. Schools or classes can trade newsletters and other correspondence.

The Historical Newspaper
By G. Grupe and R. Steffes

Why?

The production of an historical newspaper provides an authentic review of the material covered in a unit. Writing an historical newspaper gives students an opportunity to put themselves in historical situations.

Who?

Students studying history, especially those who are reluctant to write, will benefit from this activity.

How?

1. Distribute several copies of a newspaper. Invite students to get a "feel" for how the newspaper is written by looking at their newspapers and discussing various issues, such as:

   What are the various sections found in a newspaper?
   Are the sections arranged in a particular manner?
   For what purpose are the sections arranged?
   What is the style of news stories?
   How are news stories different from editorials or ads?
   How do the headlines relate to the stories?
   Do stories and pictures illustrate similar things?

2. Students generate their own questions. If possible, invite a person who works for a newspaper or a journalism student to act as a resource and answer some of the questions. The discussion familiarizes students with the production of a newspaper.

3. The group decides which historical period should be covered in their newspaper. Usually it is the period they have just studied.

4. Students form groups of about five people. They elect or appoint an editor who will oversee the newspaper's production and keep students on task to meet deadlines.

5. In their groups students brainstorm the types of stories that they will use and who will be responsible for the various sections. Editors write down the responsibilities of the staff, keeping one copy and giving another to the teacher.

6. As students prepare their individual parts of the paper they will need to keep in mind the time period in which the paper is being published. Advertisements, prices, news topics, editorials, book/movie/music reviews, for example, will all be affected by the time period. Supply reproductions of articles, advertisements, and headlines from the period that will prompt new ideas and give students a sense of the time period.

7. When all parts are completed in rough draft form, the groups begin revising and editing. They write titles, captions, and headlines; and then place all parts in final form. The paper can be typed or hand printed in predetermined column widths.

8. Upon completion of final drafts, distribute scissors and rubber cement and begin the "paste up." Students decide where the stories, ads, editorials, weather, and other sections will be located. After the "paste up" the newspaper is ready to be shared with others informally or to be displayed.

Then What?

1. Students in literature classes can write a newspaper covering events in the piece being studied.
2. Science classes can write newspaper articles covering what they find in experiments.

Crime and Causes
By L. H. Trickey

Why?

Students know that crime is a major social problem in the United States and that the media reports alarming stories daily. However, many students give little thought to the numerous social, political, and personal factors that are the causes of crime. This activity helps students to think of crime problems as something other than a "black-and-white" issue. It also encourages them to read the newspaper and to move from newspaper articles to written essays.

Who?

This activity is for upper-level secondary students in sociology, psychology, or American government.

How?

1. Students divide their notebooks into two sections by use of thumb tabs. On the front they write *Crime and Causes*.
2. Students review the newspaper each day for seven days looking for examples of crime and possible causes of crime. They cut out any article related to crime and place it in chronological order in the first half of the notebook.
3. In the second half of the notebook students place all articles concerning social or political conditions that may contribute to crime. These may be articles about hunger, poverty, overcrowding, racism, social injustice, poor educational opportunities, unemployment, child abuse, and so on.
4. Using their notebooks as references, students write a short essay on crime and its causes. This can be done collaboratively.
5. After students have completed their papers, there is a general class discussion. A line is drawn down the middle of the board; on one side of the line write the crimes listed by the students from their notebooks. On the other side list the "causes" students found.

Then What?

Students can monitor television news and compare the coverage to that in the newspaper. The images presented on television can be compared to images derived from reading about the same event in the newspaper.

Predictable Titles

By M. Henrichs

Why?

Active readers enter texts with predictions about what they are reading and why. These predictions are based on information such as where the print is located, graphic display, and organizational features such as columns and headings. The titles of newspaper articles provide information about the content and can be used to prepare readers to read.

Who?

This activity is for passive readers who don't utilize on and off the page context in making predictions.

How?

1. Choose newspaper articles with predictable titles—those which accurately reflect the content of the article. Remove the titles from the articles.
2. Students choose a title for the article and discuss what it is about.
3. List students' predictions and discuss other information that could be in an article with this title. Students can write their own articles to go with the title.
4. Students read the article and compare it with their predictions. They also identify the information in the article that wasn't predictable from the title.

Then What?

1. Students are divided into groups and each student receives a title. Each lists title predictions on paper. Titles are rotated, with each student writing a prediction for each title. After rotation, students discuss their predictions for each title; and the student holding the title adds the group responses to the list of predictions. Articles are given to students to read and match with their titles.
2. Other types of texts can be used, such as textbooks and magazines with section headings and short stories.
3. Students can divide texts into sections and come up with their own titles for each section based on content.
4. Students can be given titles and asked to guess the source of the title from a list of possibilities; then they read the respective pieces.

This Land Is Your Land

By P. Crowley

Why?

Students in American government classes can confront the ideals and realities of our political system by monitoring and reflecting on the news. Access to information is free to us and to our students by means of the media. Civics textbooks traditionally present principles of government from a predominantly theoretical point of view because the realities of the political arena are constantly changing. What is significant today is "old news" tomorrow. The study of American government comes alive when the curriculum unfolds along with the news because students can evaluate theoretical issues in light of actual events.

Who?

All students and teachers of American government can utilize this activity by drawing upon the media for valuable topics of study.

How?

1. Multiple copies of a variety of newspapers should be available, in addition to course textbooks. Students form interest groups based on the topics studied. Each group is responsible for collecting information from the daily news related to the particular topics chosen, and for discussing the information. A secretary takes notes—revolving secretaries can be used.
2. A member of each group gives a synopsis of the new information to the rest of the class during sharing time. Each group keeps a group notebook that includes the articles collected and notes generated from discussions. These notebooks are shared. Other groups can write responses to the discussion notes.
3. Depending on the topics chosen and the events in the news, some groups will follow ongoing stories (an election, for example), while others monitor changing topics (such as crime stories). Possible topics and activities include:

Elections

Follow the election of a public official.
Poll teachers, administration, and staff on particular issues.
Hold mock elections; give campaign speeches.
Hold a debate on a controversial topic.
Describe the ideal president (governor, mayor, and so on).
Study the historical precursors of current events (slavery and apartheid, for example).
Compare campaign promises to policy.

Taxes (The newspaper is not needed for these activities.)
Students fill out their own income tax forms or a form for hypothetical workers.
Teachers "audit" students if they have filled out their income taxes incorrectly. You can also play the role of tax lawyer and consult with students who need extra help.

Others
Follow a bill as it becomes law.
Follow a trial.
Chart weather changes.
Evaluate advertising and propaganda.
Study fact and opinion using the editorial page.

Then What?

1. Students can write letters to the editor of the school or local newspaper and to Congresspersons.
2. Students can monitor the television news at home and report back to the class. Discussions may center on the different reporting styles between television and print media.
3. A class government can be formed. This government can be an actual decision-making body or a simulation of the political processes being studied.

Truth Is Stranger Than Fiction

By D. Pyle

Why?

The inside pages of daily newspapers are full of short articles about unusual events and people. A collection of such stories can be kept on hand to stimulate individual or group writing.

Who?

Students who need help getting a writing project started will benefit from this activity.

How?

1. Reproduce and distribute copies of a short newspaper article, such as the one included below. Discuss ways the article could be expanded to create a short story or play.
2. Pre-writing can include acting out the event as reported; writing from the point of view of one of the people involved in the event; or producing written, oral, or drawn descriptions of the characters and setting. Invite students to create a complete story or play.
3. Various news stories will lend themselves to various types of discussion and writing. The one included here seems to be for character development and analysis of point of view: What did Mr. Harrington do and think during his ordeal? Should the niece be depicted as hysterical or calm?

Then What?

Great stories can be started with marriage announcements or personal ads. What are the stories behind the professional skier who announces her engagement to an orthopedic surgeon, or an ad that reads: "Dear Tina—We love and miss you. Please come home. Love, Mom and Dad"?

Man Survives on Taffy, Water*

WENDELL, Mass. (AP)—A half-pound of saltwater taffy and an empty beer can used to scoop up water from brooks kept a 79-year-old man alive for seven days in the woods after he became lost while taking a drive in the country.

Two loggers found Arthur L. Harrington, a retired maritime engineer who suffers from hardening of the arteries which sometimes causes him to become disoriented, Monday near the Quabbin Reservoir at New Salem.

"I never thought I'd see him again," his niece, Gladys M. Powling of Wendell, said Tuesday. "I just stood there flabbergasted."

Harrington, who had quadruple bypass heart surgery in November, endured heavy rain and chilly nights without medication for his heart condition. A medical examination after he was found showed his heartbeat had quickened from lack of medication and he had lost about 10 pounds from his 160-pound frame, but was otherwise in good health, Powling said.

*Burlington (VT) *Free Press*, Aug. 7, 1985.

Student-Generated Publications

By R. Steffes and G. Grupe

Why?

The discussion of process writing by Donald Graves (1982), Donald Murray (1968), and others has influenced many teachers. Terms like rehearsing, drafting, revising, and editing are becoming familiar in classrooms. Classroom publications of student writing show students that their work is valued and gives them an opportunity to share their writing with others. Publishing need not be difficult. A "publication" can be a student-generated magazine, written, produced, and distributed by the class.

Who?

Publishing writing benefits writers in all content area classes.

How?

There are many different ways to publish student work. Among them are:

1. Enlist students' help. They select their favorite pieces to be published, and divide responsibilities such as typing, copy-editing, illustrating, and distributing. The staff can be changed for each publication, giving everyone at least one turn on the crew. Each student's selected work is published at least once during a semester.
2. Publishing can involve students reading pieces aloud on an "Author's Day." Students can record their responses on cards and pass them back to the authors.
3. Selected pieces of writing can be displayed on a bulletin board in the classroom, in the hall, or at any "special event" such as "Back to School Night" for parents or at fund-raising events at the school.
4. Many schools have a newspaper that contains news about the school and athletic events. Why not change to a literary magazine? Instead of school news, students can enjoy short stories, poems, essays, cartoons, photographs, and reviews written by themselves, their peers, and their teachers. Entries can be submitted to a review board that selects, edits, and puts the magazine together.

Then What?

Class books or booklets can be made easily and can be inexpensively duplicated. Other kinds of publications include newspapers of a specific time period (see Strategy 7.4, for example), a gossip magazine featuring some of the characters in books read, poetry digests, short story anthologies, fictional diaries of adventurers, famous explorers, or literary characters.

Demystifying Time, or What Can You Learn in Five Minutes?

By M. Bixby

Why?

Students in classes that require extensive reading often say that they cannot comprehend what they read. This activity involves active reading: anticipating, predicting and confirming, questioning and the use of interrogatives, rapid review of print, and reading for a purpose.

Who?

Students in secondary classes who are having difficulty handling a large amount of reading will benefit from this activity.

How?

1. Give students a section of a newspaper and give them a short time to read a number of the articles in that section—the time allotted and the number of articles depend on the students involved. At the end of the time they write the important information that they remember.
2. Give students the front page of another section of the newspaper. They look at each headline and think of two to three questions from the headlines that can be answered by reading the article. For example, if a headline reads: "Evacuation Postponed at Center," they can look for answers to:

   What center?
   What kind of evacuation?
   Postponed for how long?
   Why was it postponed?
3. After students have written their questions, give them a short time to skim the article for important information, and then time to write responses.
4. Students meet in small groups and discuss their strategies, their effectiveness or ineffectiveness, their questions, and so on.

Then What?

Discuss how this sort of pre-reading can be applied to textbooks. You may have to do a bit of urging to get students to predict and question. They will usually conclude that the strategies listed above can facilitate comprehension and may make their reading demands easier.

New Ways for Old Kits

By D. Fisher

Why?

School storage closets often contain "reading kits" and related paraphernalia that have fallen into disuse. This activity suggests an alternative use for such materials that is consistent with a whole language program.

Who?

This activity benefits students who need to know that they can use written material for their own purposes.

How?

1. Review the stories, looking for those with predictable language and story lines suitable for extended literature lessons. Also look for stories (fiction or nonfiction) that can be bound and used to support classroom units (see Strategy 4.2). Students choose several stories to examine and evaluate. They fill out an evaluation card on each story. For example:

Title of story: _____
Would you recommend this story to someone else? _____
Why or why not?_____

    You will soon get an idea of the stories that students enjoy. Pull these out and cut off the "skills" pages. Now you have a variety of student-chosen stories on many subjects, printed on sturdy cardboard.

Then What?

1. Gather stories into Skinny Books. Categorize stories according to common subjects. Punch holes in the pages and collect them in a three-ring binder and house them in the class library as additional resources.
2. Students can use a story as the basis for a play. They can develop scripts, dialogue, and stage directions. Provide time and an audience for the dramatization.
3. Students can use the story to "Clone the Author" (J. Harste, 1979). With a partner, students read the selection, then take 5 × 7 note cards and write one major impression from the story on each. The impression cards are then arranged in the way students think fits the story. Students note their arrangements, then give cards to their partners and try to reconstruct their partners' arrangements. Partners discuss the arrangements.
4. Students can use the books for Schema Stories (see Strategy 5.5).

8

Extended Literature

Literature is more than well-arranged syntax that clarifies our thoughts. It is purposeful language that provides us with pleasure and understanding. There is an obvious difference between reading "Stopping by Woods on a Snowy Evening" by Robert Frost and "Snow in the Arctic Circle" from *National Geographic*. Both can provide us with information and vicarious experience, but the poem invites us to personalize the text, to reflect on our part in the "scheme of things," and to explore the nature of human existence. Mythology, fantasy, fiction, folktales, poetry, and other kinds of literature are rich sources that assist us in understanding ourselves and others.

The pleasure of literature need not end when the last page is read. This section focuses on the need for continuing involvement in further reading and writing. The following activities invite students and teachers to extend the ideas encountered in literature into personally meaningful experiences. Literature can be the connection between perception and expression. One can live through the feelings and expressions of others to experience a unique understanding of self and of the environment.

Many of these activities, such as "The Land Where the Ice Cream Grows" (see Strategy 8.4) and "Poor Richard" (see Strategy 8.10) use particular literary references. However, teachers are encouraged to develop their own procedures for using and extending all types of literature in a variety of ways.

□ Strategy □ 8.1

"The Hitchhiker," or Know Where You're Going

By D. Pyle

Why?

Most stories written in narrative style grab the reader's attention by weaving a series of interesting events around a central plot "thread." Part of the pleasure of reading is following this thread to discover an outcome. Good readers use the clues provided by the details of such stories to participate in the narrative flow. "The Hitchhiker" by Roald Dahl is a tightly structured humorous story that encourages readers to guess the occupation of a secretive, but engaging, second character along with the first-person narrator. The story can be used to demonstrate how prediction aids comprehension.

Who?

Students of all ages who have difficulty predicting story outcomes will benefit from this demonstration.

How?

1. Read the story aloud. There are several natural breaks in the narrative that can be used to invite students to participate in the guessing game. As the story progresses, and clues to the hitchhiker's occupation accumulate, a record of the author's clues and the students' predictions can be kept on the chalkboard.
2. After the story has been read, review the clues embedded in the story and discuss how they helped students monitor their interest and understanding.

Then What?

1. Follow this activity with presentation of stories or articles that are less obviously "set up" for guessing than "The Hitchhiker." Help students find textual features that provide clues to story outcome or the author's purpose.
2. Two stories by Shirley Jackson, "After You, My Dear Alphonse" and "Charles," can be used to demonstrate predictability of narrative events.

Group Courage

By D. Pyle

Why?

Emphasizing the social nature of the reading process can help reluctant readers experience the pleasure of reading a whole book without frustration.

Who?

Reluctant readers of junior high age, who have trouble staying with a book to completion, will enjoy this shared reading activity.

How?

1. *Call It Courage* by Armstrong Sperry is a short novel about a young Polynesian boy who leaves home in a small boat to prove to his village that he is not afraid of the ocean. The book is written in five chapters that describe discrete episodes in the boy's journey. This activity requires either dismantling several paperback copies of the book or photocopying.
2. Divide the class into five groups, a group for each chapter of the book, and provide copies of appropriate chapters to each member of each group.
3. Each group will read only one chapter of the book and be responsible for retelling the chapter to the rest of the class. Individual groups can prepare for this activity by shared reading of the assigned chapter or by individual reading and follow-up discussion. Group members share ideas about the best way to present their parts of the book. In one classroom it was decided in advance that each group would devise a written summary with illustrations on large sections of newsprint. When these sections were connected, they formed a mural that illustrated the entire book. Dramatic interpretation is another possibility.
4. To retell the story effectively each group must decide which events and details should be emphasized in the retelling to make the story cohesive. For example, in the classroom mentioned above, the Chapter 2 group decided it would be important to illustrate that the chapter ends with the moon rising and the boy falling asleep because it was predicted (correctly) that Chapter 3 would begin with a description of a new day. Students will need to determine when it will be helpful to explain Polynesian vocabulary that is used in the book.
5. After the contents of each chapter have been revealed to the entire class, facilitate a discussion of the advantages or disadvantages of reading a book in this way. Allow time for students to question each other about any missing pieces of information or unclear ideas.

Then What?

Students who find this activity beneficial can look for partners for shared reading of other books.

Note: Since *Call It Courage* involves a setting unfamiliar to many North American students, the teacher may wish to involve the class in pre-reading activities that will help establish a sense of Polynesian culture and geography. The teacher can introduce strategies for dealing with foreign words and phrases in context.

Colorful Reading

By P. Crowley

Why?

Through literature, students explore the many ways of seeing and knowing the world. *The Rainbow Goblins* by Ul de Rico is a fantasy about a group of colorful little creatures that "climbed the highest mountains looking for the rainbows, and when they found one, they caught it in their lassoes, sucked the colours out of it and filled their bellies with its bright liquid." The colorful language and illustrations offer opportunities for exploring sensory images (see Strategy 6.6).

Who?

This activity is for students who need experiences with figurative language.

How?

1. Before reading, discuss rainbows that the students have seen. Brainstorm how a rainbow might sound, smell, feel, and taste.
2. Begin the book by looking at the cover (which shows the goblins grabbing a rainbow in their lassoes and the colors draining into their buckets) and discussing what the book might be about.
3. Read the story to the class, allowing them to enjoy the illustrations. After reading the book, students look through a series of index cards and choose one:

   Describe a new rainbow. It can have a different shape, colors, size, smell, and so on. You may draw a picture of your rainbow, too.

   In the movie *The Wizard of Oz*, Dorothy is swept up by a tornado to the Land of Oz on the other side of the rainbow. Write a story about what you might find on the other side of the rainbow.

   The Rainbow Goblins gives a reason why rainbows never touch the earth. Write another story about rainbows which gives a different reason.

   Make up a song or poem about rainbows.

   Using the flavors of the rainbow, make up a recipe and tell how it will taste.

   Make a book of your own with your drawings about rainbows.

   Describe what you think the personality of each rainbow goblin might be like. You may want to look in the book to remind yourself of what it says about each goblin.

   Your own idea . . .

   Note: Be sure plenty of colored pencils, markers, and construction paper are available.

Then What?

1. Decorate the classroom with the writings and illustrations.
2. Each student can go to the library and choose a fantasy book to read.
3. Read *Hailstones and Halibut Bones* by Mary O'Neill. Each poem is about a different color. Write and illustrate "color" poems.

The Land Where the Ice Cream Grows, or Consumable Materials

By D. Fisher

Why?

Picture books can be resources for secondary school teachers. *The Land Where the Ice Cream Grows* by Anthony Burgess and Fulvio Testa, for example, can encourage creative thinking and writing by enabling students to see how an author experiments with language and by giving them the opportunity to play with language themselves.

Who?

Secondary students will benefit from this literary spark to thinking and writing.

How?

1. Begin by appealing to students' imaginations through guided fantasy. Before reading the story students relax and take an imaginary trip to a fantasy "Foodland." In this land there is an abundance of their favorite food. Guide the imaginative visit by asking:

   What do you see?
   What do you smell?
   How does the food taste?
   Is there anyone else there?
   Are there any problems in your special land?

2. Students write nonstop for ten minutes about their experiences in the imaginary land. This encourages the use of good descriptive words. These writings can be edited by students at a later time and collected and bound into a class book for sharing with others.

3. Read *The Land Where the Ice Cream Grows* aloud. Discuss the author's use of ice cream imagery: the "Mocha Mountains" and "Pistachio Peaks." Discuss the diary format and the way the days of the week are renamed: "Fryday," "Shattersday," "Sundae," "Munchday," and so on.

4. Give students options for related writing activities or let them choose their own:

   Make your own Foodland book with illustrations.
   You are chased by one of the giant sundaes. How do you escape?
   Use Ice Cream Land to plan a travel brochure. Name the land and use pictures and words to encourage people to visit your land.
   Imagine you are stranded on the ice creamberg in the middle of the chocolate sauce sea. How did you get there? What will you do? Does someone save you? Write and illustrate.
   Choose any subject that interests you—cars, movies, animals, and so on. See if you can change the names of the days of the week so they fit the subject.

Keep a diary of the actual happenings in your life for one week. Then pretend to be someone else—a movie star, a famous race-car driver, a wealthy business person, and so on. Keep a diary showing what this person does each day for one week, and then compare the two diaries.

Then What?

1. Collect information about ice cream, such as the history of ice cream (encyclopedia), a recipe for making ice cream (cookbook), when and why the sundae was invented (magazine). Students take the combined information and write a class story about ice cream.

2. As a culminating activity, written directions can be created for making a wonderful ice cream concoction. Each student can bring ingredients for these creations. One person can read the directions while the others make the dessert. Not only is this a good way to read and follow directions, it is a tasteful way to enjoy a class.

Extending Tales

By B. Savage

Why?

Students can use fairy tale themes in a variety of ways. The sense of justice portrayed and the humor in such tales, for example, can enhance students' understanding of the tales.

Who?

Secondary students in English literature or composition classes will benefit from this activity.

How?

Several types of activities are suitable for extending fairy tales:

1. *Monologues*—students can produce monologues in several forms. As speakers, they may address an audience at large or a specific audience.

   The troll talks to himself about his plot to control the bridge.
   Cinderella writes to her pen pal across the kingdom about her situation.
   Goldilocks talks to a newswoman as she flees the bears' house.
   A citizen of Hamelin writes a letter to the editor complaining about the rat problem.

2. *Dialogues*—students can produce dialogues that are taped or written in dramatic form.

   Two or more of the seven dwarfs complain about the lack of a housekeeper.
   The three pigs meet the three bears on a bus.
   Rumpelstiltskin talks to a judge about legally changing his name.
   Red Riding Hood talks on the telephone to her cousin Cinderella.

3. *Newspapers-Newscasts*—learners can use a media format to express understanding from an objective third-person point of view. Either a newspaper format or an oral news broadcast form can be used. These can be written, audiotaped, or videotaped.

   News articles—palace officials are stymied, since the princess cannot be awakened; local girl is reported living with a group of midgets.
   Classified ads—for sale: one slightly used grandma costume; wanted: live-in cook, contact Grumpy.
   Recipes—poisoned apples, porridge, pig soup.
   Real Estate—haunted castle, gingerbread house, small cottage in wooded setting.
   Dear Abby—my mother keeps talking to a mirror . . .; my two stepsisters are always. . . .

Then What?

1. Students can write a new fairy tale.
2. Students can dramatize monologues or dialogues for another class.
3. Students can produce a class newspaper substituting classmates' names for the fairy tale characters.
4. Use other stories for this activity, such as Aesop's *Fables* or James Thurber's *Fables for Our Time*.

□ Strategy □
8.6

Poetry

By S. R. Crenshaw

Why?

Poetry is an art that invites the reader or listener to appreciate the rhythm and beauty of language while contemplating the meaning of the imagery. Appreciating poetry involves more than the study of technical terminology and structured meter. It involves an emotional awareness and an intellectual understanding of life. Learning takes place when the thought and language of the poet combine with the experience of the reader or listener to create a sensory response. Louise Rosenblatt (1978) describes this transaction as the "lived through" experience.

Who?

All students will benefit from expanding their appreciation of language and imagery through the study of poetry.

How?

In this chapter there are several activities that are based on the use of particular poems. You are urged to develop your own procedures for the use of poetry. A general strategy lesson includes the following:

1. *Predict*—look at the title. Invite students to suggest the possible theme or author's intent.
2. *Listen*—read the poem aloud several times. This may be a shared reading by you, the students, partners, or other combinations.
3. *Savor*—students read the poem silently to note the sensory allusions or the striking metaphors.
4. *List*—suggest a listing of images noted.
5. *Question*—to assist the awareness activity, some questions can serve to encourage responses:

   What did you see, hear, smell, taste, feel?
   What did you think about?
   Did it remind you of anything or anyone else?
   What do you think the author was trying to say?
6. *Share*—There are many possibilities such as:

   Illustrating the poem with a compatible setting.
   Expressing ideas in poetic form.
   Extending an idea, feeling, desire, or image generated by the poetry.

Then What?

1. Students can study the backgrounds of particular poets.
2. Students can keep a poetry journal noting ideas and reactions about particular feelings.
3. A poetry book would contain favorites of individuals and contributions of student writing.

Know Nothing Situations

By S. R. Crenshaw

Why?

Humor, fear, absurdity, and other related topics abound in literature. Students can draw on their own experiences to understand and enjoy these topics better when they appear in literature.

Who?

Students who need encouragement to express humor, fear, or personal anxieties based on their backgrounds and experiences will benefit from this activity.

How?

1. Shel Silverstein's poem "Wild Boar" (1981) ends with the thought that the speaker knows nothing about the number of teeth in a wild boar's mouth. Talk about ridiculous, fearful, or embarrassing situations that students know nothing about but are certain they want to avoid.
2. Individuals or partners devise such a situation and illustrate the problem. Emphasize content, not artwork. Share the drawings with partners and invite them to guess the problem. Students then write about their problems and create solutions. Before the solutions are revealed, ask other students either to write or tell what they would do.

Then What?

1. Focus on the positive approach and suggest an activity that stresses happy situations: "Things I'm glad I know something about." Feelings, tastes, sights, and sounds are possible themes. The literary forms may be as varied as the subjects.
2. Find related literary works that illustrate the sorts of humor, fear, or absurdity that learners have described.

The Rest of the Story

By S. R. Crenshaw

Why?

Literature sparks the imagination and invites readers to become writers. Engaging readers with text that draws them into personal responses and reactions extends their language experiences.

Who?

Reluctant writers will benefit from using poetry to get them started in writing.

How?

1. Read "Suspense," a short poem by Shel Silverstein. The last line teases the imagination by saying that he has forgotten the rest of the story. The plot of the poem is like an old melodrama.
2. The "rest of the story" may be related to radio commentator Paul Harvey's features. Talk about some possibilities for interesting endings.
3. Direct students to write endings, either individually or in groups, and to share them with the rest of the class. After editing and typing, suggest colorful illustrations to accompany them. Collect the various story endings and make a class book.

Then What?

1. Rather than finishing the story, students can stop at a suspenseful point and pass the text to someone else to add another episode. It can become a serial or continuing story by adding new characters and situations.
2. The idea can also be dramatized with costumes and sets for presenting to other groups.

Dying to Write

By committee

Why?

Students need opportunities to read and enjoy a variety of types of poems in order to appreciate the many forms, styles, and topics that comprise that genre. This activity uses poems that tell stories.

Who?

Secondary students in literature, American studies, history, or other content area classes will benefit from this activity.

How?

1. Initiate discussion with questions such as:

   What do you know about _____'s (name of town) history?
   Do you have relatives who have lived and died here?
   Can you think of places, streets, buildings named after famous local people?
   Do you know or remember any family stories that have to do with the history of _____ (name of town)?

2. Read "Lucinda Matlock" in *Spoon River Anthology*. Students browse and read from *Spoon River Anthology*.

3. Bring in newspaper obituaries and discuss the kinds of information found in epitaphs and obituaries. Students write their own epitaphs or obituaries.

Then What?

1. Students can take a trip to a cemetery and do charcoal rubbings.
2. Students can write epitaphs or obituaries for fictional characters in literature or for historical figures, or they can participate in a thematic unit on death and dying.

| ☐ Strategy ☐ |
| 8.10 |

Poor Richard

By R. Steffes

Why?

This activity is designed to use poetry to motivate discussion of current issues related to personal life situations. The statistics concerning suicide are an impetus for dealing with the problem.

Who?

This activity can be used in junior high, senior high, and with college students.

How?

Read "Richard Cory" by E. A. Robinson and provide copies so that students can follow. Students write their immediate reactions, then discuss what their feelings are concerning the poem. Focus on ideas that they particularly liked or disliked, as well as the characterization of Richard Cory and the reasons for his suicide.

Then What?

1. Based on students' reactions, discuss the problem of suicide.
2. Discuss the clichés "the grass is always greener on the other side" and "you can't judge a book by its cover" as they apply to the poem and to society.
3. Examine how the person "inside" can differ from the one projected to others.

Powerful Poetry

By M. Henrichs

Why?

Poetry enriches the classroom experience. Students respond to poetry when it relates to issues that touch their personal lives. This strategy lesson is designed to stimulate discussion of appearance versus reality.

Who?

This activity can be used with secondary literature students.

How?

1. Read Auden's "Unknown Citizen" aloud, and distribute copies of the poem to the students to read silently.
2. Place the following topics on the board:

   Examine the "Unknown Citizen" in the eyes of society.
   What does the poem mean to you?
   React to any line that particularly strikes you.
   Describe how the poem makes you feel.
3. Group students for discussion with a secretary to take notes in each group. Students discuss their notions and compare these with the ideas of other group members.
4. Following group discussions, the secretaries summarize what was said in their groups. A class discussion follows in order to compare, contrast, or synthesize the ideas from the small group discussions.

Then What?

Students read "Richard Cory" (see Strategy 8.10), comparing and contrasting the characters and themes in this poem and in "Unknown Citizen."

Tripping on Poetry

By S. R. Crenshaw

Why?

Poetry offers an excellent opportunity to assist students in understanding and expressing feelings about themselves and their worlds. As students experience the transaction with a text that reflects a unique sensation or an outlet of emotional expression, they are better able to understand the complexities of decision-making.

Who?

Students who need alternative learning experiences to extend their horizons through imagining, interacting, and creating other settings in order to generate writing ideas will benefit.

How?

1. Collect poetry that focuses on travel. Students do research in literature and poetry anthologies to find suitable poems to share with the class. Have a collection ready for oral reading.
2. Students imagine a place that they would most like to visit, and write a narrative about traveling to that locale.
3. Partners share writing with each other. Ask guiding questions such as:

   What did you like best about your narrative?
   Is there anything you would like to change?
   What else would you like to add?

   This gives students the opportunity to revise and share ideas.
4. Invite students to write their own travel poems and illustrate them with drawings or collected pictures from travel magazines or other sources.

Then What?

To make the transition from the imaginary to the real world, students locate a place on the map or globe and do research on the climate and geographical features. Ask them to compute the distance and decide the best mode of travel. They can plan their trips based on the information gathered.

<table>
<tr><td>☐ **Strategy** ☐
8.13</td><td></td></tr>
</table>

Take a Risk

By P. Crowley

Why?

For learning to take place, learners have to take risks, that is, to attempt tasks which are a step beyond their present performance and therefore involve the possibility of failure. To move ahead, however, students must take these risks.

Who?

Students who are reluctant to try things which are difficult for them because of the risk of failure will benefit from this strategy.

How?

1. Begin by brainstorming on what it means to take a risk. Accept all responses and discuss them. Relate the discussion to the risks which are taken in school-related situations.
2. Give each student a copy of the poem "Risks" (author unknown, see below), and read it to them.
3. Students break into small groups and assign sections of the poem to be discussed by each group. Move from group to group and monitor the discussion and make comments.
4. As a class, discuss what went on in the groups and how risks can be encouraged and taken in the classroom. Talk about reading a book which seems just a little too hard and about sharing writing.
5. Post the poem in the room and refer to it when encouraging risk-taking in the future. Praise and encouragement must be given for trying. Even if the attempt was unsuccessful, learning has still occurred.

Risks

To laugh is to risk appearing the fool.
To weep is to risk appearing sentimental.
To reach out for another is to risk involvement.
To expose feelings is to risk exposing your true self.
To place your ideas, your dreams, before a crowd is to risk their loss.
To love is to risk not being loved in return.
To live is to risk dying.
To hope is to risk despair.
To try is to risk failure.
But risks must be taken, because the greatest hazard in life is to risk nothing.
Those who risk nothing do nothing, have nothing, and are nothing.
They may avoid suffering and sorrow, but they cannot learn, feel, change, grow, love, live.
Chained by their attitudes, they are slaves, they have forfeited their freedom.
Only a person who risks is free.

Author Unknown

130

Then What?

In their journals students can keep track of the risks that they take and their results. The choice to share these experiences is available.

9

Invitations to Read and Write

In a very real sense this whole book is an invitation to read, write, and think. We have emphasized the holistic nature of language and the value of integrating the arts of listening and speaking with reading and writing.

This section includes a variety of invitations to use language through reading conferences, book searches, literary journals, book sharing, group writing, and editing procedures. Again, as in the case of the general Strategy Lessons, these invitations meet individual needs in group settings and encourage collaboration. When students and teachers collaborate in purposeful, experienced-based literacy activities, invitations are accepted and learning occurs.

| ☐ Strategy ☐ |
| 9.1 |

Ways to Help Students Find "Just the Right Book"

By F. Reynolds

Why?

Helping students choose "just the right book" for Sustained Silent Reading (see Strategy 4.1) and other pleasure reading is very important. The right book can often get a student "hooked" on reading.

Who?

All secondary school students who have not developed personal criteria for selecting books and reluctant readers who claim that they don't like reading will benefit from this strategy lesson.

How?

1. A classroom library is essential. Paperback books from a variety of genres that appeal to students of varying abilities and interests provide the opportunity for choice. Several paperback suppliers offer good discounts on books. Inexpensive sources of books include garage sales, library benefit book sales, thrift shops, and donations from students, faculty, and friends.
2. Become familiar with students' literature by reading the books and professional journals that review young adult literature. Keep a file on these books.
3. A reading interest inventory provides information about what appeals to students.
4. Suggest three or four books that might appeal to the student.
5. Let students know what you read for enjoyment. Share books you are currently reading and talk about why you like them.

Then What?

1. Ask students to share their books after Sustained Silent Reading. Give students opportunities to talk to friends about their interests and to recommend titles. After discussions about books, pass the books around for students to browse through.
2. Schedule a book fair for the entire school. Many paperback suppliers or bookstores have book fair services.

<table>
<tr><td>☐ **Strategy** ☐
9.2</td><td>## Book Searches
Adapted from B. Nelms</td></tr>
</table>

Why?

Book Searches are opportunities to become acquainted with fiction and nonfiction genres not explored previously; to use book sources in the school and community (libraries, bookstores, personal libraries, etc.) for leisurely browsing; to write short, descriptive, personal responses; and to share choices with others.

Who?

All students in any content area or language arts class can benefit from finding and sharing books.

How?

Directions to students:

1. Each week you will be asked to find (search for) a book in one of the following categories:

   A book of fiction in your favorite genre.

   A book in a subject area of interest to you.

   A good book to read aloud; cite groups for which the book would be appropriate.

   A book of fiction in a genre you've never explored before.

   A book in a subject area you would like to know more about.

   Other options—choose one:

   A book of poetry.

   A classic of literature.

   A specialized encyclopedia or almanac.

   A book or story from another country.

   An anthology (*i.e.*, short stories, myths, fables, biographies, ethnic collections, etc.).

(continued)

2. For your book search responses use a 4 × 6 card and complete:

Name
Date

Author
Title
Publisher and copyright date.
1. Briefly summarize the book.
2. Why did you choose this book, or why is it important;
who would enjoy it?

3. Your response/reaction:

---

3. Students bring their books and share them with the class.
4. For the read-aloud book search, prepare students with suggestions on reading aloud. *The Read-Aloud Handbook* by Jim Trelease has some good suggestions. Students can practice with a tape recorder before their class presentations.
5. Students pick the "best part" of their responses. These excerpts should be typed and then distributed to the class.

Then What?

The searches can be varied with each class each semester. Classes can devise their own "search" genres. Library times can be scheduled so the librarian and teacher can help.

Another Way of Using Book Searches
By D. Pyle

Why?

Reluctant readers sometimes feel uncomfortable when trying to find a book to interest them. Shopping for a book for someone else, though, can help students learn the organization of the library and expose them to a variety of subjects that might otherwise be ignored. This is a good activity for getting acquainted with the library and fellow students at the beginning of the school year.

Who?

Students who are unfamiliar with the organization of the library or who have trouble choosing books will benefit.

How?

1. Students complete a brief questionnaire about their interests and experiences. Another way of getting this information is to invite students to interview each other.
2. When the questionnaires are completed, redistribute them among the students so that each has some information about a classmate. Students go to the library to shop for at least three books of various types for a fellow student. It might be helpful to have students make a list of subjects and genres appropriate to the questionnaire each holds before going to the library.
3. After students have searched the library and selected titles, the books are brought to the classroom for presentation to their recipients. The books are presented with either oral or written explanations as to why they were selected. For example: "I chose this book about engine repair for you because you said you liked working on your motorcycle."
4. After students have received their books, they discuss orally or in writing their reactions to the selections made for them.

Then What?

1. This activity is a way to observe students' perceptions of their reading ability and their familiarity with printed materials.
2. Shopping expeditions can be repeated throughout the school year by individual students to welcome transfer students or in response to events in students' lives ("Tim just got a car! Who wants to go book shopping?").

You Can't Judge a Book by Its Cover

By C. Gilles

Why?

Reluctant readers often choose short books because they fear that longer ones will be difficult. This activity helps them approach a wider variety of books.

Who?

Students who have difficulty choosing a book or those who consistently choose short, controlled-vocabulary books will benefit from this strategy lesson.

How?

1. Read aloud a conceptually complex children's book, such as *The Golden Serpent* by Walter Dean Myers, without letting the class see the cover or pictures.
2. Discuss the story with the students, drawing them toward inferential meaning by using questions such as:

   What do you think the old man is really looking for?
   What do you think the golden serpent symbolizes?

   Students suggest a "grade level" or a "reading level" for the book.
3. Read a selection for a "high interest," controlled-vocabulary series, such as those from Xerox Publications or Fearon Publications. One example is Xerox's *The Red Ghost*. Discuss the story and ask for a possible grade level.
4. Students write about which book they would rather read and why. Most students will choose the more sophisticated children's book because the language is natural and engaging and the plot is sensible.
5. Show students the covers of both books. Discuss the concepts of grade level and reading level, as well as what to look for when selecting a book. These issues are related to more than the length of the book or the picture on the cover.

Then What?

1. Students can choose a passage out of each book and compare the language choices. Talk about language. Is a shorter sentence generally easier or harder to read? Does the length of a word have anything to do with its difficulty?
2. Students can react to both books and share these reactions with each other. This can lead to a discussion about the "levels" of books.
3. Students can look for passages in books (including textbooks) that are difficult to read because the author used unfamiliar or ambiguous wording. These passages are copied and posted in the classroom for discussion of reading strategies appropriate for each.

Reading Conferences

By F. Reynolds

Why?

Reading conferences between students and teachers can be enjoyable experiences that encourage reading choices and help measure students' progress in their reading. Conferences provide opportunities to discuss problem areas, and to suggest appropriate strategies and other reading material that might be of interest to students. Conferences help the teacher get to know the students.

Who?

Students in language arts or content area classes benefit from the interaction provided by reading conferences.

How?

Students

1. Keep a list of your reading, citing the title, author, and date completed.
2. Write a response about the book. Do not just summarize the plot, but write about how you think and feel about what happened in the book.
3. When you complete a book, schedule a conference with your teacher.

Teachers

1. Read (or at least skim) as many books that your students read as is possible, or read book reviews in *The Horn Book, English Journal, ALAN Review,* and so on.
2. Keep a card file.
3. Schedule reading conferences with the students on a regular basis. They can be called conferences or Book Talks or whatever suggests a good conversation about reading and books.
4. Keep the conference casual and nonthreatening. The following list of questions might be helpful:

Questions about the Book in General

Tell me what you read, in your own words; or What was the story about, briefly?

What were some of the problems (conflicts) in the story? Why were they problems (conflicts)?

What was your opinion of the book? Did you like it or not? Why?

What were the qualities of the book that made it (good, enjoyable, interesting, educational, and so on) for you?

How could you have made the book better?

If you could change any part of the book in any way, what would you do?

Compare this book with others you have read either by the same or another author?

What were some of the turning points in the story?

Questions about the Characters

How do you think the characters felt in a certain situation (name incident)?

How did the character(s) change from the beginning to the end of the story? Why did they change?

What would you have done if you had been the character? Why? Has anything like this ever happened to you? How could the situation be changed?

How does the main character in the story compare to the main character in the last book you read (or read by the same author)?

If you met the main character (or one of the other characters) in the story in person, what would you ask him or her? Or, what would you say or do?

Which character in the book did you like the best (or least) and why?

Would you like to trade places with any of the characters in the story? If so, which one and why?

Which character would you like to have as a friend?

Questions on the Quality of Writing or Other Literary Merits

What part of the story was hardest for you to understand? Let's go to that part of the book and talk about what puzzled you.

What would you have changed about the ending of the story? Why?

Would you like to meet the author? If you could, what would you talk about or what advice could you give?

Is there any part of the story that you would have left out in order to make it more interesting? If so, what part and why?

Would you read another book by the same author?

Did you think the book was well written as far as use of language was concerned?

Questions on the Relationship in the Book to the Reader's Own Life

Are there any characters in the book who are like you?

What did you learn from this book? Something about people? New ideas? Something about the time period?

Do you believe that everything in the book could have happened? Why or why not? Was the story intended to be true to life?

Did anything happen in the book that is similar to something that happened to you or someone you know?

Can you compare this book to another book or article you have read?

Conference Evaluation

Conferences can be evaluated as follows:

1. No grade at all.
2. Credit given for a satisfactory or excellent conference depending on the nature of the discussion.
3. Evaluation based on levels of response as follows.

   The student knows about the plot, characters, conflicts, setting of the book (i.e., "This book is about a young man who hoped to make it big in the boxing world. He worked hard and at the end he almost won the title bout.").

The student makes some personal comments about the plot, characters, conflicts, setting, and makes some connections to his/her own life, other reading, learning, or experiences (*i.e.*, "My uncle tried prizefighting once. I know he trained very hard. But he never made it to the top as he didn't have the will to win like the guy in the book did. This also reminds me of *The Contender* by Robert Lipsyte.").

The student extends the ideas or theme of the book into other areas of life (*i.e.*, "I think that any time a person tries to make it big in sports they not only have to have talent but a lot of perseverance. I'm not sure that the fame and fortune would be worth the physical trauma of a boxer.").

The student evaluates the book in some way (*i.e.*, "This was a great book! I could really get into the guy's head because the descriptions were so real and I felt I was boxing along with him. The language used was very gutsy—just the kind you would expect to find in a gym.").

Inference—Extension of Meaning

By M. Henrichs

Why?

Some students are unable to go beyond the literal interpretation of the text. They cannot "read between the lines" and infer levels of meaning. This strategy lesson, through the use of teacher and student questioning, helps readers to monitor their cognitive thinking and to expect multiple meanings.

Who?

This strategy lesson is especially beneficial to those students who have difficulty seeing more than one interpretation for a passage.

How?

1. Collect various types of writing that have more than one meaning. These can be short passages, poems, political cartoons, entries from student journals, and so on.
2. Demonstrate to students how you would question and respond as you read the piece. Try to verbalize the mental procedures that you go through as you read. For example, in the poem, "Afraid" by Langston Hughes:

We cry among the skyscrapers
as our ancestors
cried among the palms in Africa
Because we are alone,
It is night,
And we're afraid.

   You might first question the title: "I wonder what he or she is afraid of?" Other statements might range from commenting about the comparisons between skyscrapers and palms to the similarity between night in a part of Africa and night in a big city. Demonstrate to students what you think about, question, and ponder as you read.
3. Ask students to help you come to one "meaning" based on your reading aloud and reflecting. They will soon discover that there are many meanings that can be made of that very short poem.
4. Students read the next piece silently and monitor their own mental proceedings. They note on paper the most obvious meanings, and then the unstated ones.
5. Students form into groups and share their entries. One person in the group acts as secretary and records the different meanings that various individuals have attached to the passage.
6. Students then reread the passage and see if the interpretation changes after group interaction.
7. A general class discussion follows the small group work. The secretaries share the various small group meanings. Discussion centers on the nature of multiple layers of meaning and how a person's background affects the meaning that is constructed.

Then What?

Students may write individual or collaborative texts which attempt to draw on reader inference. Writings are exchanged, and readers question and note the various layers of meanings that they have constructed.

□ Strategy □ 9.7

Recreational Reading

By M. Henrichs

Why?

This reading strategy lesson acquaints the reluctant reader with literature in a motivating way.

Who?

This activity is enticing for students who say that they "hate to read."

How?

1. Select a paperback novel of general interest and provide appropriate background information in an overview of the book in order to set the mood for reading.
2. The book is separated by chapters and each student is responsible for reading one or more chapters.
3. Act as the moderator while students retell their chapters, contributing information as needed.
4. The students write their reactions to the book and discuss these in small groups. These are later shared with the entire group. They can discuss the interrelatedness of the different sections, characterization, theme, and so on as well.

Then What?

1. Students can write an expanded reaction paper and share these in groups for peer revision. These papers are kept in the classroom to share with other students who read the book.
2. The students are invited to write reactions to books they read independently and to share these with others.

Dealing with Dialogue
By D. Loyd

Why?

Students frequently encounter dialogue in text. Reading dialogue in professionally authored texts helps students see how such authors use it. Writing dialogue gives students opportunities to develop plot and character traits through dialogue.

Who?

Students who have difficulty interpreting dialogue in literature and students who are interested in using conversation in their writing will benefit from this strategy.

How?

1. Use comic strips to illustrate different types of dialogue. Make copies of strips with the balloons whited out. Students create the dialogue appropriate for the situation shown. Students may wish to draw their own cartoons or comic strips to make class books. Be sure to use comic strips that have enough information to reconstruct a story.
2. Photographs or slides showing groups of two or three people can be used. Students describe the people and situations: Where was the picture taken? What might the people be talking about in such a situation?

Then What?

1. As a class or in small groups students examine a story or section of a novel or short story that contains dialogue. They discuss how the author uses dialogue to illustrate character traits, to identify the speakers, and to develop the plot.
2. Students break into groups, describe a situation, and write dialogues for the characters in the situation. The groups switch papers and decide whether or not the conversation seems natural in the particular context described. If not, students make the revisions they feel are necessary and then pass the conversation to another group for peer editing. After all revisions are made, the conversation can be acted out in a skit.

Wordless Books for Secondary Students

Adapted from Y. Goodman and C. Burke

Why?

Although teachers usually associate wordless picture books with young children, they can be used at a secondary level to help students predict and confirm and to develop a sense of story.

Who?

This activity is valuable for reluctant readers, reluctant writers, and students who have difficulty predicting and relating what they read to their own experiences.

How?

1. Select several wordless books (see resources below), and pick one to read and discuss. Students predict what the stories are about, based on the pictures. Several students in the groups can take turns telling their stories.
2. Each student picks a book for which to write (or audiotape) the text. They trade books and texts, read each other's stories, and discuss their stories. You can type various scripts to be placed around the room or in a class library.

Then What?

1. Students can work in pairs using the same books.
2. Students can use a Written Conversation format (see Strategy 4.4) with one book. Each student takes turns writing the story.

Wordless Books for Secondary Students

Author	Book
Anderson, Laurie	*The Package*
Anno, Mitsumasa	*Anno's Animals*
	Anno's Britain
	Anno's Journey
	*Dr. Anno's Magical Midnight Circus**
	Italy
	Topsy Turvies: Pictures to Stretch the Imagination
Asch, Frank	*George's Store*
	Linda
	The Blue Balloon
Brinckloe, Julie	*The Spider Web*
Carle, Eric	*I See a Song*
	The Very Long Train
Carroll, Ruth	*The Dolphin and the Mermaid*
Giovannetti	*Max*

Goodall, John S.	An Edwardian Christmas
	An Edwardian Holiday
	An Edwardian Summer
	Shrewbettina's Birthday
	Story of an English Village
	The Ballooning Adventure of Paddy Park
Hamburger, John	The Lazy Dog
Krahn, Fernando	A Flying Saucer Full of Spaghetti
	The Great Ape
Mayer, Mercer	Frog Goes to Dinner
	Oops
	Two Moral Tales
Mordillo, Guillermo	The Damp and Daffy Doings of a Daring Pirate Ship
Ringi, Kjell	The Winner
Shulevitz, Uri	Dawn*
	Treasure*
Spier, Peter	Noah's Ark*
Turkle, Brinton	Deep in the Forest
Vasiliu, Mircea	What's Happening
Ward, Lynd	The Biggest Bear*
	The Silver Pony
	The Wild Pilgrimage
Wetherbee, Holden	The Wonder Ring: A Fantasy in Silhouette
Wetzel, Peter	The Good Bird
Wildsmith, Brian	Brian Wildsmith's Circus

*These books are not wordless, but they have easily covered script.

□ Strategy □
9.10

Book-Sharing through Written Conversation
Adapted from C. Burke

Why?

When students are required to write book reports, the importance of a personal response to text is diminished. When students are required to report only the facts of a book, it implies that books are for reporting and that there is one "main idea" to be found in the text. However, when students interact with one another in sharing books, the focus is on what is important to them and why. Since students are aware of the interests and experiences of other students, they can tap information that would probably not appear in a book report.

Who?

It is valuable for all language users to discuss books with their peers.

How?

After students have read a book of their choice, they break into groups of two or more. They are to "discuss" their books through Written Conversation (see Strategy 4.4). There is no talking allowed; the entire discussion is written. All students have a chance to discuss the books they read.

Then What?

Written Conversations can be available as resources for choosing books in the future.

Patchwork Story
By C. Van Camp

Why?

Developing awareness of predictability in story schema—the elements and progression of stories—enhances clear, interesting writing. It also encourages predicting what might happen next in a story.

Who?

Students who need a structure or impetus for story writing benefit from this activity, as well as students who are reluctant to predict events in stories they read.

How?

1. Students begin writing a story of their choice, establishing setting, characters, and a beginning to the plot. Set a timer for two or three minutes.
2. When the timer rings, students change seats (clockwise, row by row, and so on). Everyone moves and begins writing on the paper at the next desk. They are to read the previous text and add to it. Continue this procedure until students are back at their own desks.
3. Students write a conclusion to the story they started. Each person can take a turn reading the patchwork story aloud. Class discussion can focus on the way the different parts of the story fit together, and how the story progresses and changes.

Then What?

The class can discuss how particular professionally authored stories are organized. The beginning of a professionally authored story can also be used in this activity. Students then read the rest of the original story and discuss similarities and differences between their stories and the original.

Descriptive Writing

By T. Mitze

Why?

Written language is enhanced when students become aware of the functional aspects of writing. This activity is designed to involve the student in the following activities:

Translating the perception of an abstract image into written language.
Writing descriptive paragraphs.
Following written directions.
Communicating with a partner through the use of written language.

Who?

All students will benefit from gaining insight into the relationship among thinking, writing, listening, reading, and speaking.

How?

1. Find various detailed figures that can be drawn on the board or projected on an overhead (for example: flags, art objects, a yin-yang symbol, and so on).
2. Prepare students to write by demonstrating the procedure. Draw a figure on the board and then write a paragraph describing it. The physical description should be detailed enough for someone else to be able to picture the object.
3. Divide the class into two teams with partners in each and send half of each team out of the room or have them turn their desks around. Draw one of the figures on the board, or display it on an overhead. The students in the room or facing the board write their descriptions. Some may be familiar with the function or symbolism of the object, while others may only have access to its physical characteristics.
4. Remove the figure and ask the other half of the class to read their partners' paragraphs and attempt to draw the figure. Repeat the procedure with the students switching roles.

Then What?

Discuss ways in which symbols operate in written language and in visual representations. Can these always be translated?

| □ **Strategy** □ | **Picture This!** |
| 9.13 | *By S. Twaddle* |

Why?

This activity provides students with an opportunity to write descriptively, and stimulates discussion on stereotyping.

Who?

Readers and writers needing encouragement in writing expressively and descriptively will benefit from this activity.

How?

1. Collect pictures of people who appear to be from different ethnic backgrounds, social classes, occupations, and so on.
2. Individuals or pairs of students select one picture, make predictions about the personality behind the picture, and compose a paragraph or story describing their characters.
3. Students read their descriptions, while others guess which picture is being described.

Then What?

Use this activity as a starting point for a discussion of this topic. Appropriate stories include "The Ransom of Red Chief" by O. Henry and "The Alligators" by John Updike.

How Do You Spell . . .?

By P. Crowley

Why?

It is a common misconception that one learns to spell by memorizing word lists. Considering the number of words that the average child can spell by early school age, this is an impossibility. Words mastered on a weekly spelling list often fail to carry over into students' spontaneous writing, because memorizing isolated words is a decontextualized activity limited to its own purposes, not to the production of meaningful written language.

When students are allowed to write, they use their intuitive knowledge of symbol-sound relationships to invent their own logical spellings (Chomsky, 1970; Read, 1975). As students use written language expressively and receptively, their spellings approach standard form and their storehouses of standard spellings increase. At times, the transition to standard spelling involves the consideration of spelling on a conscious level—looking at spelling for spelling's sake.

Using standard orthography is a courtesy to the reader and can be incorporated naturally into the writing process.

Who?

All students involved in the writing process develop spelling strategies.

A Caution: Some students, particularly those who have difficulty with spelling, put too much emphasis on spelling. They may feel that they cannot write if they cannot spell. It is important that spelling be de-emphasized with these students because their concern for spelling negatively affects their production of written language—and therefore their spelling. Students should be comfortable and confident about the content of their writing before they concern themselves with the mechanics of writing.

How?

1. After a student has chosen a piece to take to publication and content revisions have been made, there are a number of strategies for dealing with spelling:

    Published writing, both student authored and professionally authored, should be visible and available in the classroom.

    Before students go outside of themselves for help on spelling (for example, by asking someone or looking in a dictionary), they should be encouraged to identify those words that are not in standard form and to try to spell them a different way.

    Human resources and published resources, such as dictionaries and thesauruses, should be available to support authors. Encourage students to use these resources as proficient writers do: to confirm predictions. Too often, students are expected to "look it up" rather than to make educated guesses about the spelling of a word, drawing on their own linguistic repertoires.

Take on the role of editor and put the spelling in standard form for publication.

Students take turns as peer editors responsible for working with other student authors in preparing their final drafts for publication.

Short mini-lessons (five to ten minutes) on spelling rules that are fairly regular (such as "*i*" before "*e*" except after "*c*"), spelling variations (such as the variant spellings and meanings of *there, their,* and *they're*), or other orthographic information (such as the use of the apostrophe in the formation of possessives) are valuable when taught at times when the information is applicable to the editing situation.

Discussion of etymology and word formation can be of interest in discussions about language.

Students can keep personal dictionaries for words that give them difficulty.

Then What?

This list of strategies is by no means complete. It merely serves to emphasize that the processes of reading and writing are the best spelling teachers.

Teachers Write Too

By P. Crowley

Why?

Because much of what students read is edited and published writing, they don't always have a sense of the process that went into creating those pieces. Students sometimes believe that an author's first effort appears in published form.

Teachers of writing must be writers themselves. Taking part in writing for real purposes not only legitimatizes the activity in the students' minds but helps teachers be empathetic to the frustrations and joys that come from writing. When students see adult writers involved in the process, they develop greater awareness of the various components of the process. This awareness can lead to more active involvement in their own writing.

Who?

All students of writing will benefit, particularly those who don't think that proficient writers work through a series of drafts.

How?

1. Present a written piece that involved multiple drafts. Share each of the drafts and describe the mental processes involved in the various stages of the production of the piece. The drafts can be shared by using an overhead projector to recreate the original process or simply to display each draft.
2. Students offer suggestions at points where decisions can be made about the outcome of a draft. Discuss the alternatives, evaluating the choices made by the author as well as how choices might differ depending on the purpose of the piece.

Then What?

1. The focus of the discussion can be on a particular aspect of the piece, such as imagery, order, reference, dialogue, and so on.
2. Keep a file containing various types of writing such as poetry, reports, and business letters, and all of the artifacts involved in their production (such as notes, scratched-out sections, arrows, rewrites—everything).
3. Discuss misconceptions about the idiosyncrasies of writing. Students sometimes hear such things as: "The best place to write is at a desk with absolute quiet." This may be true for some writers, but others may write best sitting on the floor with the radio on. Students should be allowed to develop their own idiosyncrasies. Leaving these pragmatic choices to the writer, you can concentrate on helping students work through the mental processes involved in writing.
4. Write with the students whenever possible, contributing to the atmosphere of a writing workshop.

Group Writing: Emphasizing Student Skills in Composition

By R. Steffes and G. Grupe

Why?

Group writing aids students in the production of quality papers as they go through the writing process. By using this approach students remain confident in their writing abilities, learn writing strategies from each other, and feel a sense of pride in their accomplishments when the pieces are completed.

Who?

Students who dread writing (those who have difficulty putting their thoughts into words) and those students who write well but have trouble with organization or generating ideas will benefit from this activity.

How?

1. This approach works best when taking a piece of writing to publication after drafting, revising, and editing.
2. Students review several pieces of their writing, and pick one for group writing. Match students according to their particular strengths in composition. A student who is full of ideas can work with one who is a good editor. A student who has difficulty getting started can be matched with a good editor and a prolific writer. Students use their individual strengths to support each other in collaborative writing.

Then What?

Student writing can be published in a variety of ways (see Strategy 7.9).

10

Computers and Whole Language Instruction

■ Computer-Assisted Instruction

An important question that must be answered regarding the use of computer-assisted instruction is: What can computers do that other forms of instruction address less adequately? More specifically, in terms of this book the question is: Can a whole language program be enhanced by the use of computers?

Examination by the authors of hundreds of titles of computer software programs has resulted in disappointment. We, as teachers, have been cautious in bringing computer programs into the classroom, in part because we perceive the inadequacy of existing programs. However, despite the paucity of good available programs, there are some exceptions worth noting. Many programs, already in use, may be modified by the creative teacher. Heads must come out of the sand on the computer issue, for computer-assisted instruction appears to be a fact of contemporary educational life. Teachers need to become familiar with the software in their disciplines in order to have a voice in the purchase of programs, to modify or use an existing program, and to be able to express a knowledgeable rejection to much of the current existing software. A great amount of surrounding material needs to be used in conjunction with a computer program.

A program can only offer facts. It is the students' interaction with and reaction to the program that facilitates thinking, reasoning, and finally learning. Thus, the teacher's role becomes increasingly important. And as the teacher's role takes on a new dimension in computer-assisted instruction, so does that of students. While teachers must provide and orchestrate the learning environment, it is often the students who provide the greatest source of computer knowledge for the teacher. Students may well be the classroom experts in computer use, and the motivational aspects of such use cannot be denied. Nor can the collaborative aspects of computer instruction be ignored. Computers do not cause isolation of students; in fact, they bring interested students together to share information and discuss outcomes. Since whole language programs are student centered, where the teacher is also a learner, it is in keeping with the philosophy of this book to examine various categories of computer-assisted instruction and their possible value for whole language instruction.

Computer use has been organized in several arbitrary categories. Some commonly used functions include gaming/simulation, drill and practice, information retrieval, tutorial, and word processing.

In general, we feel that gaming devices are best left outside the classroom. Carefully chosen simulations, on the other hand, may enhance a whole language content area classroom when used in conjunction with other learning sources. Drill and practice is currently the most prevalent use of computers in education; and, perhaps, it is the most dangerous because much nonsense has been transferred from ditto sheets and workbooks to software. In addition, an excessive reliance on testing for drill and practice programs may have impeded the development of better educational software and fostered a false notion that learning actually takes place in this manner. Selected tutorial programs for content areas are worthy of consideration, and informational retrieval systems, such as spelling checks and vocabulary generation, are valuable as instructional aids. The word processor offers endless possibilities for creative, collaborative activities.

Activities

Computers used in conjunction with teacher-designed activities have the potential to enhance the whole language classroom. Activity centers or stations appear to be useful in classroom organization. For whatever purpose the computer center is engaged—be it a collaborative pre-writing activity, drafting or revising a paper, a simulation requiring logical thinking, graphics, music or math tutorial, or for countless other uses—it should be seen as but one of several classroom activity areas. Other areas in the whole language classroom might include a journal entry center, as well as stations for reading, listening, discussion of related topics, and typing. Again, we emphasize the notion of teacher judgment, familiarity, and creativity in the implementation of computer software programs.

Many of the preceding whole language strategies included in this book would be adaptable and perhaps enhanced by the appropriate addition of computer software programs. For example, Written Conversation (see Strategy 4.4) might easily utilize a word-processing program for the initial activity and for all of its variations. Extensions of the Wordless Books for Secondary Students (see Strategy 9.9) could be a computer collaborative effort. Students might work in pairs at the computer in order to write a script. A graphics package could be used to generate on-line wordless books, and a script could be created for these graphics.

Computer graphics could also be used to extend the Sketch to Stretch strategy lessons (see Strategies 5.4 and 6.9), as well as Colorful Reading (see Strategy 8.3). Word-processing programs could be used with such strategies as Extending the Newspaper (see Strategy 7.3). Computer use could extend all of the strategies in the section on poetry (see Strategies 8.6–8.13). Students might also enjoy collaboration in poetry writing by using a program designed for the computer.

Studying

Studying is a unique and focused form of reading. The computer has unlimited potential as a study aid. In a review of the current literature on studying,

Anderson and Armbruster (1986, p. 674) stated that "almost any study technique can be effective if it is accompanied by focused attention. . . ."

■ Software Programs

Computer programs capture the attention, interest, and imagination of students. Reading, writing, listening, and speaking activities in content areas may be developed from existing school software. The teacher must decide what software programs assist whole language instruction and how to utilize these programs in the classroom. At times it may be necessary to disregard the package's procedures and objectives in order to examine the program in terms of its fit in whole language instruction.

It is beyond our intent to recommend specific commercial software programs, but we do feel that teachers who understand and embrace whole language principles will find the conversion or modification of existing available programs to be both challenging and rewarding. Software available in the public domain and that are available through computer users' groups may likewise highlight instruction and learning in whole language content classrooms. For example, if student partners use a history simulation program, they can discuss the historical outcome; they can do research on the event in any number of related areas; and they can write expository or creative papers based on their findings. In addition, they can lead group or class discussions related to the historical period.

We have found both school and public librarians to be knowledgeable and helpful in our search for content area software with whole language application. We have also found that the time used for examining software catalogues and looking at available school programs was time well spent. Appropriate use of computers does help to focus student attention and thus aids learning.

■ Computer as Part of Whole Language Program

The computer can be used as part of the whole language classroom. Since computers appear to be here to stay, we should neither ignore them nor be intimidated by them; instead we must become computer-wise. This knowledge will enable us to utilize existing programs, to reject programs of questionable educational merit, and to have a voice in the development of future educational software programs. We need to be involved with computer application committees in our schools, where we will continue to be learners as well as teachers as we explore the exciting potential of computer use for whole language classrooms.

Easy Writer—Computers and the Writing Process

By F. Reynolds

Why?

Word-processing programs for personal computers lend themselves well to whole language activities in any secondary school classroom. All phases of the writing process can be facilitated by computer. It seems to lessen writing blocks and gives many students their first true successes with writing. Using a word processor can show a student that writing is the communicating of a message, not just simple surface features like correct spelling and handwriting. If some students and/or the teacher do not know how to use a word-processing program there are usually other students who do and who are more than delighted to show off their expertise. This can provide an opportunity for the teachers to demonstrate that they too are learners.

Who?

All students in any content area classroom will benefit from using word processing.

How?

Materials: Computers, word-processing programs like Applewriter, Appleworks, Bank Street Writer, PFS Writes, MECC Writer, and FreeWriter (the last three are the easiest to learn initially but limited in some ways).

1. Introduce students to the word-processing program. If some students already know how to use a computer and word-processing program they can be encouraged to work with those who don't (including the teacher). Make sure that all students know how to use floppy disks and use the computer itself.
2. After any pre-writing activities (brainstorming, listing, library research, reading, and so on) students start their rough drafts using the programs of their choice. Continue to work in pairs or small groups so the "experts" can help the others. Printouts of rough drafts are easy to obtain. Corrections are made on the printouts, then on the monitor; or students can edit on the screen and then print.
3. Other revisions and editing can also be done in the same manner. One of the spelling programs can be used during editing.
4. Final copies can be printed out, and multiple copies can be made for class books or for groups to use in their reading.

Then What?

1. When students have achieved proficiency on a word-processing program they usually can't be kept away from a computer. They are eager to write and will usually "plunge" into a writing assignment without the usual reluctance.

2. Written Conversations (see Strategy 4.4) are fun to do on a computer. These can be used as a way of learning how to use a word-processing program, or can be the rough drafts of a play or skit.
3. Collaborative writing (see Strategy 9.16) in any form can be done on the computer.

Evaluating Computer Software—A Checklist

By F. Reynolds

Why?

Computer software is expensive, so it is very important to have procedures to evaluate it before purchase. Some companies will send examination copies to schools; other programs may be examined in a computer software store. It is very important to try out a software package and to peruse the manual for clear and coherent directions before purchasing. If possible, let some students try it out to get a "second opinion."

The following checklist may be reproduced and used when evaluating software educational programs. However, since no one checklist can provide all the criteria to judge a particular program for a specific group of students, it is important to add criteria that fit your particular needs.

Checklist for Evaluating Educational Software

Title of Program: _____

Subject of Program: _____ Age or Grade: _____

Manufacturer/Distributor: _____ Cost: _____

Computer System Required: _____

Number of Disk Drives Needed: _____ Memory Required: _____

Reviewer: _____ Date: _____

Y e s	N o	N / a	

			I. Compatibility
			   A. Is compatible with teacher's beliefs about curriculum, learning, and learner?
			   B. Is compatible with systems in use, including printer?
			II. Directions
			   A. Are directions self-explanatory and easy to read?
			   B. Are instructions controlled by user? (User determines when instructions disappear from screen.)
			   C. Can user return to instructions during program?
			   D. Is set of abbreviated instructions constantly displayed on screen?
			   E. Is program menu-driven?
			   F. Does computer use "English" messages, not computer jargon?
			III. Documentation
			   A. Is documentation available for software?
			   B. Does documentation include a list of the software capabilities?
			   C. Does documentation include a tutorial for novice user?
			IV. Program Design
			   A. Will it motivate and interest the age group intended?
			   B. Does it allow for collaboration?
			   C. Does it allow for choices?
			   D. Is it relevant to actual tasks?
			   E. Are instructions clear for students?
			   F. Is it easy to correct typing mistakes?
			   G. If input is entered incorrectly, does computer give example and ask user to try again?
			V. Additional Comments:

Program Rating:

_____Pass

_____Pass reservations

_____Fail

Further Reading—
The Computer
in the Classroom

Bridwell, L., Johnson, P., and Brehe, S. (1985). Composing and computers: Case studies of experienced writers. In A. Marsuhaski (Ed.), *Writing in real time: Modeling production processes*. N.Y.: Longman.

Bruce, B., Michaels, S., and Watson-Gegeo, K. (1985). How computers can change the writing process. *Language Arts, 62* (2), 143–149.

Collier, R. (1983). The word processor and revision strategies. *College Composition and Communication, 34*, 149–155.

CRLA (*Computers Reading and Language Arts*, a professional journal). P.O. Box 12039, Oakland, CA 94661.

Journal of Reading, International Reading Association, 800 Barksdale Road, P.O. 8139, Newark, DE 19714. (Usually has review of software in each issue.)

Leahy, E. (1984). A writing teacher's shopping and reading list for software. *English Journal, 73* (1), 62–65.

Marling, W. (1983). What do you do with your computer when you get it? *Focus: Teaching English Language Arts, 9*, 48–53.

Oliver, L. (1984). Pitfalls in electronic writing land. *English Education, 16* (2), 94–100.

Papert, S. (1980). *Mindstorms: Children, computers and powerful ideas*. N.Y.: Basic.

Rodrigues, R. (1984). The computer-based writing program from load to print. *English Journal, 73* (1), 27–30.

Standiford, S., Jaycox, K., and Auten, A. (1983). *Computers in the English classroom*. Urbana, IL: NCTE.

Schwartz, H., and Bridwell, L. (1984). A selected bibliography on computers in composition. *College Composition and Communication, 35* (1), 71–77.

Zinsser, W. (1983). *Writing with a word processor*. N.Y.: Harper.

References for Part II

Adler, M., and VanDoren, C. (1972). *How to read a book.* N.Y.: Simon and Schuster.

Anderson, T., and Armbruster, B. (1986). Studying. In P. D. Pearson (Ed.), *Handbook on reading research* (pp. 657–679). N.Y.: Longman.

Atwell, M. (1980). *The evolution of text: The interrelationship of reading and writing in the composing process.* Unpublished doctoral dissertation, Indiana University, Bloomington.

Aesop (1978). *Aesop's twenty fables.* N.Y.: Doubleday.

Attenborough, R. (Director) (1983). *Gandhi* (Videotape, Columbia).

Auden, W. (1950). "Unknown Citizen," *Collected Shorter Poems.* London: Faber and Faber.

Burgess, A., and Testa, F. (1979). *The land where the ice cream grows.* Garden City, N.Y. Doubleday.

Burlington Free Press. (Staff). (August 7, 1985). Man survives on taffy, water. Burlington, VT.

Calkins, L. (1985, October). Paper presented at the Mid-Missouri Teachers Applying Whole Language Renewal Conference, Columbia, MO.

Corn, A. (1982). Combining the 3 R's: Using whole language skills in elementary math. *Missouri Schools, 47* (7), 19–21.

Dahl, R. (1979). The hitchhiker. In *The wonderful story of Henry Sugar and six more.* N.Y.: Bantam.

deRico, U. (1979). *The rainbow goblins.* N.Y.: Warner.

Eanet, J., and Manzo, A. (1976). REAP: A strategy for improving reading/writing/study skills. *Journal of Reading, 19* (8), 647–652.

Forbes, E. (1943). *Johnny Tremain.* Boston: Houghton Mifflin.

Gaines, E. J. (1971). *The autobiography of Miss Jane Pittman.* N.Y.: Dial.

Gregory, D. (1964). *Nigger.* N.Y.: Simon and Schuster.

Gilles, C. (1982). E.R.R.Q.—A comprehension based strategy. *The Missouri Reader, 7* (2), 4–6.

Glossbrenner, A. (1984). *How to get free software.* N.Y.: St. Martin's.

Goodman, Y., and Burke, C. (1980). *Reading strategies: Focus on comprehension.* N.Y.: Richard C. Owen.

Goodman, Y., Watson, D., and Burke, C. (1987). *Reading miscue inventory: Alternative procedures.* N.Y.: Richard C. Owen.

Gould, G. (1959). Wander-thirst. In Mayhill and Arbuthnot Collection, *Time for Poetry,* (Rev. ed.). Glenview: Scott, Foresman.

Graves, D. (1982). *Writing: Teachers and children at work* Exeter, NH: Heinemann.

Guthrie, J. (1983). Scientific literacy. *Journal of Reading, 27*(3), 286–288.

Harste, J. (1985). Clone the author. In Harste, J., Pierce, K., and Cairney, T. (Eds). *The authoring cycle: A viewing guide.* Portsmouth, NH: Heinemann.

Harste, J., Pierce, K., and Cairney, T. (Eds.) (1985). *The authoring cycle: A viewing guide.* Portsmouth, NH: Heinemann.

Henry, O. (1953). *The complete works of O. Henry.* Garden City: Doubleday.

Hughes, L. (1926). "Afraid," in *The weary blues.* N.Y.: Knopf.

Hoffman, S. (1983). Using student journals to teach study skills. *Journal of Reading, 26* (4), 344–347.

Hunt, I. (1970). *No promises in the wind.* N.Y.: Grosset & Dunlap.

Jackson, S. (1982). After you, my dear Alphonse; and Charles. In *The lottery and other stories.* N.Y.: Farrar, Straus, Giroux.

King, M. (1963). "I have a dream." Copyright by Martin Luther King, Jr.

Korty, J. (Director). (1981). *The autobiography of Ms. Jane Pittman.* N.Y.: RCA.

Krahn, F. (1978). *The great ape.* N.Y.: Viking.

Langer, J. (1981). From theory to practice: a pre-reading plan. *Journal of Reading, 25* (2), 152–156.

Lawrence, R. (1979). *North runner.* N.Y.: Holt, Rinehart and Winston.

Lipsyte, R. (1967). *The contender.* N.Y.: Bantam.

McCracken, R. (1971). Initiating sustained silent reading. *Journal of Reading, 14* (81), 521–524 and 582–583.

Manzo, A. (1975). Guided reading procedure. *Journal of Reading, 18* (4), 287–291.

Manzo, A. (1969). The ReQuest procedure. *Journal of Reading, 13* (2), 123–126.

Masters, E. (1925). Lucinda Matlock. In *Spoon River anthology.* N.Y.: Macmillan.

Mowat, F. (1963). *Never Cry Wolf,* N.Y.: Franklin Watts.

Murray, D. (1968). *A writer teaches writing: A practical method of teaching composition.* Boston: Houghton Mifflin.

Myers, W. (1980). *The golden serpent.* N.Y.: Viking.

O'Neill, M. (1961). *Hailstones and halibut bones.* Garden City: Doubleday.

Orwell, G. (1946). *Animal farm.* N.Y.: Harcourt.

Otfinoski, S. (1977). *The red ghost.* N.Y.: Xerox.

Rico, G. (1983). *Writing the natural way.* Los Angeles: J.B. Tarcher.

Robinson, E. (1956). "Richard Cory." In *The American tradition in literature* (3rd ed.). N.Y.: W.W. Norton.

Rosenberg, B. (1982). *Genreflecting—A guide to reading interests in genre fiction.* Littleton: Libraries Unlimited.

Sanacor, J. (1983). Improving reading through prior knowledge and writing. *Journal of Reading, 26* (8), 714–720.

Sanders, A. (1985). Learning logs, a communication strategy for all subject areas. *Educational Leadership, 42* (5), 7–8.

Scholastic Scope (Eds.). *Imagination: The world of inner space* (1970). New York: Scholastic Book Services.

Siegel, M. (1984). Sketch to stretch. In *Reading as signification.* Unpublished doctoral dissertation, Indiana University, Bloomington.

Silverstein, S. (1981). Suspense. In *A light in the attic.* N.Y.: Harper & Row.

Silverstein, S. (1974). Hector the collector; Sarah Sylvia Cynthia Stout would not take the garbage out; Wild boar. In *Where the sidewalk ends.* N.Y.: Harper & Row.

Sperry, A. (1940). *Call it courage.* N.Y.: Macmillan.

Stevenson, R. (1905). Travel. In *A child's garden of verses.* N.Y.: Scribner's.

Suhor, C. (1982). *Reading in a semiotics-based curriculum.* Urbana, IL: (ERIC Document Reproduction Service No. ED 215-299).

Taylor, M. (1976). *Roll of thunder, hear my cry.* N.Y.: Dial.

Thurber, J. (1954). *Fables for our times and Famous poems.* N.Y.: Harper & Row.

Time (Staff). (July 8, 1985). "Immigrants."

Trelease, J. (1982). *The read-aloud handbook.* N.Y.: Penguin.

Updike, J. (1964). The alligators. In *Olinger stories, a selection.* N.Y.: Vintage.

Vacca, R. (1981). *Content area reading.* Boston: Little, Brown.

Watson, D. (in press). Skinny books. *Language arts ideas for elementary children.* Urbana, IL: NCTE.

Watson, D., Robinson, R., and Chippendale, E. (1979). The Burke Reading Interview modified for older readers. In *Describing and improving the reading strategies of elderly people.* Columbia, MO: University of Missouri, Joint Center for Aging Studies.

Whitman, W. (1967). "The open road." In *Complete poetry and selected prose and letters.* London: Nonesuch.

Appendices

APPENDIX A

Parents Are a Support System in the Reading Process

Learning to read is not a goal that is realized at the end of first or second grade—it is an ongoing process. Reading at the secondary school level should focus on lifetime pleasure as well as the importance of acquiring information. Parents can be supportive by setting examples through sharing reading and writing experiences.

Communication with parents is essential in building a supportive environment. Contact with parents takes many forms; suggested book lists, informal notes sent home, phone calls, conferences, and classroom newsletters are possibilities.

1. A booklist for recommended reading includes references such as:

   Books and the Teenage Reader: A Guide for Teachers, Librarians, and Parents (2nd revised edition) by G. Robert Carlsen, published by Harper and Row.

   Books for You: A Booklist for Senior High Students, edited by Kenneth Donelson, published by National Council of Teachers of English.

2. A letter to parents could include suggestions such as:

   Focus on reading which includes a variety of reading material readily available for leisure and family reading time. Demonstrate that reading is valuable beyond school requirements. Include a daily newspaper and one or more magazines or journals in the family budget.

   Develop an accepting attitude that values choices of reading material. Show an interest in what your adolescents are reading, and accept their miscues. When they confront unfamiliar material, encourage them to continue reading; the context usually strengthens their predictions. Allow them to self-correct. Mispronouncing, omitting, or substituting words may indicate that a reader is trying to make sense of the text. This is a strength, not a concern.

   Extend reading experiences by taking turns in choosing materials for shared reading. Ask the young adults for their suggestions. Take time to talk about areas of agreement and disagreement. Reading each other's selections can be mutually beneficial.

Keep a journal or a reading reaction log. A journal or log is valuable for recording reactions, ideas, and questions for later discussion—or for further reading.

Give books as gifts. Encourage family members to make thoughtful selections for themselves, friends, or relatives. Spend time in the library to review new books and materials as good possibilities for gift-giving. Librarians and bookstore personnel are valuable resources for choosing books.

Display reading materials. Utilize books, magazines, journals, art works, and other materials as a part of your home. Vary the selection and arrangements to increase curiosity and interest. Accessibility is a definite advantage.

3. Phone calls and conferences with parents are helpful. Invite them to share their experiences and perhaps submit short reviews for a classroom newsletter.

4. Parents are a great resource. Ask them to come to the classroom and talk about their interests in particular areas. Invite their suggestions for expanding the curriculum in meaningful ways.

When students and parents find connections among their interests and in their reading and writing, everyone benefits.

APPENDIX B

Burke Reading Interview

By C. Burke (1987)

Name _____ Age _____ Date _____

Occupation _____ Education Level _____

Sex _____ Interview Setting _____

1. When you are reading and you come to something you don't know, what do you do? Do you ever do anything else?

2. Who is a good reader you know?

3. What makes him or her a good reader?

4. Do you think that she or he ever comes to something she or he doesn't know when she or he is reading?

5. If answer is YES: When she or he does come to something she or he doesn't know, what do you think she or he does about it?

If answer is NO: Suppose _____ comes to something she/he doesn't know. What do you think she/he would do?

6. If you knew that someone was having difficulty reading, how would you help that person?

7. What would a/your teacher do to help that person?

8. How did you learn to read? What did they/you do to help you learn?

9. What would you like to do better as a reader?

10. Do you think that you are a good reader?

APPENDIX C

Textbook Handling Interview

By M. Bixby and D. Pyle

Reader _____

Class _____

School _____

1. You're assigned a chapter in this book. What would you do when you approach the assignment for the first time?

   Do you ever do anything else?

2. If you knew someone was having trouble with this text, how would you help that person?

3. Do you think you get all the information you need?

4. What would you like to do better in regard to textbook handling?

Additional Comments

APPENDIX D

Writing Strategies Interview

Adapted from P. Atwell's 1979 version
by M. Bixby

Name _____

Date _____

1. When you are writing and something stops you, what do you do?

   What might stop you when you are writing?

   Do you ever do anything else?

2. If you knew someone was having trouble writing, what would you do to help?

3. What would a teacher do to help him or her?

4. You have been told you have to write an essay due in one week. What will you do?

5. Who do you know who is a good writer? What makes him or her a good writer?

6. Do you think she or he ever gets stopped when she or he is writing?

_____ YES _____ NO

Why?

What does she or he do about it?

7. What kinds of things do teachers tell you to help you write well?

8. What is the best advice you've ever been given about writing?

9. How did you learn to write? When? Who helped you?

10. What would you like to do better when you are writing?

11. Do you think you are a good writer? _____ YES _____ NO

Why?

12. Do you ever draw when you write? _____ YES _____ NO

 Which do you do first, usually?

 How does drawing (help, affect) your writing?

 How does writing (help, affect) your drawing?

13. What are people's purposes for writing?

 What are your purposes for writing?

APPENDIX E

The Class Interview

Adapted from the Burke
Reading Interview (1987) by M. Bixby

Name _____

Class _____

1. What subject areas do you read with the most ease? Name two.

   What are the most difficult things you have to read? Be specific.

2. What subject area or areas will you have to read the most to finish school?

3. What courses are you taking this semester? How are you doing in each class?

4. What kind of reading/study skills do good students possess? (For example, notes, test-taking, organization, and so on.)

On the other hand, what kinds of study/reading skills do poor readers have?

5. When you are reading and you come to something you don't know or that gives you trouble, what do you do?

6. When a good reader is reading and she or he comes to something unfamiliar or troublesome, what does she or he do?

7. What would you like to do better as a reader?

8. What do you read routinely for pleasure? How frequently?

9. What is the most memorable thing you've ever read?

10. Are you comfortable with your writing (not handwriting) ability? Why or why not?

11. What aspects of your writing would you like most to improve? Be specific.

Bibliographies

BIBLIOGRAPHY A

Theory-based Bibliography

What do classroom teachers need to know about language development, linguistics, and cognitive processes? The answer is as much as possible, since these processes build a bridge between an occasionally successful Monday morning and the development of a sound program of instruction based on what linguists, cognitive psychologists, and educators tell us about how learners use language. The following titles represent a continuum of thought about learning and language and present ideas that inform, encourage, and enrich the classroom teacher.

Anderson, R., Spiro, R., and Montague, W. (1977). *Schooling and the acquisition of knowledge.* N.Y.: Erlbaum.

Bartlett, F. (1932). *Remembering.* Cambridge: Cambridge University Press.

Berger, A., and Robinson. A. (Eds.) (1982). *Secondary school reading—what research reveals for classroom practice.* Urbana, IL: ERIC Clearinghouse on Reading and Communication Skills and National Conference on Research in English.

Britton, J., Burgess, T., Martin, N., McLeod, A., and Rosen, H. (1975). *The development of writing abilities (11–18).* Houndmills Basingstoke, Hampshire: Macmillan Education.

Carey, R. (1980). Empirical vs. naturalistic research? *Reading Research Quarterly, 5,* 412–415.

Chomsky, C. (1970). Reading, writing, and phonology. *Harvard Educational Review, 40,* 287–309.

Edelsky, C. (1984). *Theory and practice in two meaning-centered classrooms* (29 min. color videotape). N.Y.: Richard C. Owen.

Edelsky, C., and Smith, K. (1984). Is that writing—or are those marks just a figment of your curriculum? *Language Arts, 61* (1), 24–32.

Goodman, K. (1986). *What's whole in whole language?* Portsmouth, NH: Heinemann.

Goodman, K., Smith, E. B., Meredith, R., and Goodman, Y. M. (1987). *Language and thinking in school* (3rd ed.). N.Y.: Richard C. Owen.

Green, J., and Bloome, D. (1983). Ethnography and reading: Issues, approaches, criteria, and findings. In J. Niles and L. Harris (Eds.), *New inquiries in reading research and reading instruction* (32nd Yearbook of NRC). Rochester, N.Y.: National Reading Conference.

Gumperz, J. (1981). Conversational inference and classroom learning. In J. Green and C. Wallat (Eds.), *Ethnography and language in educational settings*. N.J.: Ablex.

Halliday, M. (1978). *Language as social semiotic*. Baltimore, MD.: University Park Press.

Halliday, M. (1975). *Learning how to mean—explorations in the development of language*. London: Edward Arnold.

Hammill, D. (1979, October 6). The field of learning disabilities: A futuristic perspective. Paper presented at the National ACLD Conference on Learning Disabilities, Louisville, KY. (Order from Donald Hammill, 8705 Merion Circle, Austin, TX 78754.)

Harste, J., and Burke, C. (1977). A new hypothesis for reading teacher research: Both teaching and learning of reading are theoretically based. In P. D. Pearson (Ed.), *Reading: Theory, Research and Practice, 26th Yearbook of the National Reading Conference*. St. Paul, MN: Mason.

Heath, S. (1983). *Ways with words*. Cambridge: Cambridge University Press.

Huey, E. (1908). *The psychology and pedagogy of reading*. Cambridge, MA: MIT Press.

Langer, J. (1984). Examining background knowledge and text comprehension. *Reading Research Quarterly, 19* (4), 468–481.

Langer, J. (1981). Prior knowledge and its relationship to comprehension. *Journal of Reading Behavior, XIII* (4), 373–379.

Langer, J., and Smith-Burke, M. (1982). *Reader meets author: Bridging the gap—a psycholinguistic and sociolinguistic perspective*. Newark, DE: International Reading Association.

Marek, A., Goodman, K., with Babcock, P. (Eds.) (1985). *Annotated miscue analysis bibliography* (Program in Language and Literacy No. 16). Tucson, AZ: Arizona Center for Research and Development.

Martin, N. (1983). *Mostly about writing—selected essays*. Upper Montclair, N.J.: Boynton/Cook.

Neisser, U. (1976). *Cognition and reality*. San Francisco, CA: W.H. Freeman.

Pearson, P. (Ed.) (1977). Reading: Theory, research, and practice. *26th Yearbook of the National Reading Conference*. Clemson, S.C.: Mason.

Shanklin, N. (1981). *Relating reading and writing: Developing a transactional theory of the writing process* (Monograph in Language and Reading Studies). Bloomington, IN: Indiana University Press.

Shuy, R. (1981). A holistic view of language. *Research in the Teaching of English, 15,* 101–111.

Suhor, C. (1982). *Reading in a semiotics-based curriculum*. Urbana, IL: ERIC Clearinghouse on Reading and Communications Skills (ED 215-299).

Vygotsky, L. (1962). *Thought and language*. Boston: MIT Press.

Wolf, M., et al. (Eds.) (1980). *Thought and language/language and reading*. Cambridge, MA: Harvard Educational Review, Reprint #14.

Wolvin, A., and Coakely, C. (1979). *Listening instruction*. ERIC Clearinghouse on Reading and Communications Skills, (ED 170 827).

BIBLIOGRAPHY B

Theory in Use—Reading and Writing

Successful teaching involves the practical application of a strong theoretical base. This bibliography contains books and articles which focus on the reading process, the writing process, and the connection between the two. Articles giving practical suggestions— such as kidwatching techniques, using trade books, and using writing to make meaning in the secondary schools—help to bridge the gap between theory and practice.

Allen, P., and Watson, D. (Eds.) (1976). *Findings of research in miscue analysis: Classroom implication.* Urbana, IL: National Council of Teachers of English.*

Applebee, A. (1981). *Writing in the secondary school.* Urbana, IL: NCTE.*

Bower, G. (1976). Experiments on story understanding and recall. *Quarterly Journal of Experimental Psychology, 28* (4), 511–534.

Britton, J. (Speaker) (1971). *Writing to learn and learning to write* [Cassette recording]. Troy State College: NCTE.*

Brown, A. (1982). Learning how to learn from reading. In J. Langer and M. Smith-Burke (Eds.), *Reader meets author: Bridging the gap—A psycholinguistic and sociolinguistic perspective.* Newark, DE: International Reading Association.

Calkins, L. (1983). *Lessons from a child.* Exeter, N.H.: Heinemann.

Calkins, L. (1986). *The art of teaching writing.* Portsmouth, N.H.: Heinemann.

Cleary, D. (1978). *Thinking Thursdays.* Newark, DE: International Reading Association.

Cooper, C., and Petrosky, A. (1975). Reading strategies and teaching implications for secondary school from the psycholinguistic model of the reading process. *High School Journal, LIX* (2), 91–102.

Crowley, P. (1983). Revision—kids helping kids. In J. Collins (Ed.), *Teaching all the children to write.* N.Y.: New York State English Council.

Donovan, T., and McClelland, B. (Eds.) (1980). *Eight approaches to teaching composition.* Champaign, IL: NCTE.*

Elbow, P. (1981). *Writing with power.* N.Y.: University Press.

Emig, J. (1971). *The composing processes of twelfth graders.* (Research Report No. 13), Champaign, IL: NCTE.*

Emig, J. (Speaker) (1973). *Why we write* [Cassette tape]. KS: Kansas Association of Teachers of English, NCTE.*

Fulwiler, T. (1980). Journal across the disciplines. *English Journal, 69* (9), 14–19.

Fulwiler, T., and Young, A. (Eds.) (1982). *Language connections: Writing and reading across the curriculum.* Urbana, IL: NCTE.*

Gilles, C. (1982). E.R.R.Q.—a comprehension based strategy. *The Missouri Reader, 7* (2), 4–6.

Gollasch, F. (Ed.) (1982). *Language and literacy: The selected writings of Kenneth S. Goodman, Vols. 1 & 2.* Boston: Routledge and Kegan Paul.

183

Goodman, K. (1973). *Psycholinguistics and the teaching of reading.* Newark, DE: International Reading Association.

Goodman, K. (1976). *Reading: A conversation with Kenneth Goodman.* IL: Scott, Foresman.

Goodman, K. (1984). Unity in reading. In A. Purves and O. Niles (Eds.), *Becoming readers in a complex society* (Part 1: 83rd Yearbook of the National Society for the Study of Education). Chicago, IL: University of Chicago Press.

Goodman, Y. (1974). I never read such a long story before. *English Journal, 63* (8), 65–71.

Goodman, Y. (1978). Kid watching: An alternative to testing. *Journal of National Elementary Principals, 57* (4), 41–45.

Goodman, Y., and Burke, C. (1980). *Reading strategies: Focus on comprehension.* N.Y.: Richard C. Owen.

Goodman, Y., and Watson, D. (1977). A reading program to live with: Focus on comprehension. *Language Arts, 54* (8), 868–879.

Goodman, Y., Watson, D., and Burke, C. (1987) *Reading miscue inventory: Alternative procedures.* N.Y.: Richard C. Owen.

Graves, D. (1981). A new look at research on writing. In S. Haley-James (Ed.), *Perspectives on writing in grades 1–9.* Urbana, IL: NCTE.*

Graves, D. (1982). *Writing: Teachers and children at work.* Exeter, NH: Heinemann.

Hansen, J., Newkirk, T., and Graves, D. (Eds.) (1985). *Breaking ground.* NH: Heinemann.

Harste, J. (1985). Portrait of a new paradigm: Reading comprehension research. In A. Crismore (Ed.), *Landscapes: A state-of-the-art assessment of reading comprehension research, 1974–1984* (Final Report USDE-C-300-83-0130). Bloomington, IN: Indiana University, Language Education Department.

Harste, J., Woodward, V., and Burke, C. (1984). *Language stories and literacy lessons.* N.H.: Heinemann.

Hasselriis, P. (1980). Sustained silent reading, an integral part of your reading program. *Missouri Schools, 45* (7), 23–25.

Jaggar, A., and Smith-Burke, T. (Eds.) (1985). *Observing the language learner.* Newark, DE: International Reading Association.

Judy, (Tchudi) S. N., and Judy, S. J. (1979). *The English teacher's handbook.* Cambridge, MA: Winthrop.

King, D. (1983). Written conversation. In J. Collins (Ed.), *Teaching all the children to write.* N.Y.: The New York State English Council.

Langer, J., and Pradl, G. (1984). Standardized testing: A call for action (Position paper prepared for the Reading Commission of the National Council of Teachers of English). *Language Arts, 61* (7), 764–767.

Ley, T. (1979). Getting kids into books: The importance of individualized reading. *Media and Methods, 17* (7), 22–26.

McCracken, R. (1971). Initiating sustained silent reading. *Journal of Reading, 14* (8), 521–524 and 582–583.

McCrimmon, J. (1970). Writing as a way of knowing. *The promise of English* (Distinguished lectures). Urbana, IL: NCTE.*

Meyer, B. (1982). Reading research and the composition teacher: The importance of plans. *College Composition and Communication, XXXIII* (1), 37–49.

Mischler, E. (1979). Meaning in context: Is there any other kind? *Harvard Educational Review, 49* (4), 1–19.

Moffett, J. (1973). *A student-centered language arts curriculum.* Boston: Houghton Mifflin.

Murray, D. (1968). *A writer teaches writing: A practical method of teaching composition.* Boston: Houghton Mifflin.

Murray, D. (1982). Teaching the other self: The writer's first reader. *College Composition and Communication, XXXIII* (2), 140–147.

Nelson, J. (1978). Readability: Some cautions for the content area teacher. *Journal of Reading, 21* (7), 620–625.

Newman, J. (1985) *Whole language: Theory in use.* Portsmouth, NH: Heinemann.

Odell, L. (1980). The process of writing and the process of learning. *College Composition and Communication, XXXIII* (1), 42–50.

Petrosky, A. (1982). From story to essay: Reading and writing. *College Composition and Communication, XXXIII* (1), 19–36.

Rosenblatt, L. (1978). *The reader, the text, the poem.* Carbondale, IL: Southern Illinois University Press.

Rosenblatt, L. (1980). What facts does this poem teach you? *Language Arts, 57* (4), 386–394.

Shuman, R. (1978). *Strategies in teaching reading: Secondary.* Washington, D.C.: National Education Association.

Siegel, M. (1984). Reading as signification. Unpublished doctoral dissertation, Indiana University, Bloomington.

Sims, R. (1972). A psycholinguistic description of miscues generated by selected young readers during the oral reading of text material in black dialect and standard English. Unpublished doctoral dissertion, Wayne State University, Detroit, MI.

Smith, F. (1975). *Comprehension and learning: A conceptual framework for teachers.* N.Y.: Richard C. Owen.

Smith, F. (1975). Twelve easy ways to make learning to read difficult, and one difficult way to make it easy. In F. Smith (Ed.), *Psycholinguistics and Reading*, pp. 183–196. N.Y.: Holt, Rinehart and Winston.

Smith, F. (1978). *Understanding reading* (2nd ed.), N.Y.: Holt, Rinehart and Winston.

Smith, F. (1979). *Reading without nonsense.* N.Y.: Columbia Teachers College.

Smith, F. (1982). *Writing and the writer.* N.Y.: Holt, Rinehart and Winston.

Smith, F. (1983). *Essays into literacy.* London: Heinemann.

Smith F., and Goodman, K. (1971). On the psycholinguistic method of teaching reading. *Elementary School Journal, 71* (4), 177–181.

Sommers, N. (1982). Responding to student writing. *College Composition and Communication, 33,* 148–156.

Tchudi, S., and Yates, J. (1983). *Teaching writing in the content areas: Senior high school.* Washington, D.C.: National Education Association.

Templeton, S. (1979). Spelling first, sound later: The relationship between orthography and higher order phonological knowledge in older students. *Research in the Teaching of English,* October (13), 255–264.

Tovey, D., and Kerber, J. (Eds.) (1986). *Roles in literacy learning.* Newark, DE: International Reading Association.

Trelease, J. (1982). *The read aloud handbook.* N.Y.: Penguin.

Walshe, R. (Ed.) (1982). *Donald Graves in Australia, children want to write.* Exeter, N.H.: Heinemann.

Watson, D. (1982). In college and in trouble . . . with reading. *Journal of Reading, 25* (7), 640–645.

Watson, D., and Bixby, M. (1985). Teachers! A support group needs you! *Georgia Journal of Reading, 10* (2), 13–17.

For further information see also various issues of the following journals:

International Reading Association:
The Reading Teacher
The Journal of Reading
NCTE*:
The English Journal
Language Arts
Research in the Teaching of English
College Composition and Communication

*National Council of Teachers of English, 1111 Kenyon Road, Urbana, IL 61801.

BIBLIOGRAPHY C

Books about Books

An integral part of a whole language program is books—GOOD books! Junior and senior high-school teachers need to incorporate into the curriculum literature that is appealing to secondary school students. The following bibliography contains lists of excellent books, as well as ideas about how to use them.

Adell, J., and Klein, D. (1976). *A guide to non-sexist children's books.* Chicago: Academy.

ALAN Review (Assembly on Literature for Adolescents), NCTE Quarterly.*

Bettelheim, B., (1977). *The uses of enchantment.* N.Y.: Vintage.

Booklist. Ongoing in *Horn Book Magazine.* Boston: Horn Book (monthly).

Books for young adults. *English Journal.* Urbana: NCTE* (monthly).

Carlsen, G. (1979). What beginning English teachers need to know about adolescent literature. *English Education, 10* (4), 195–202.

Donelson, K. (1972). *The students' right to read.* Urbana, IL: NCTE.*

Donelson, K. (1980). Spanning the decades. *Media and Methods, 16* (7), 24 and 44–47.

Donelson, K., and Nilsen, A. (1980). *Literature for today's young adults.* IL.: Scott, Foresman.

Fader, D. (1977). *New hooked on books.* N.Y.: Berkeley Medallion.

Journal of Reading. Newark, N.J.: International Reading Association (monthly).

Outlook Tower. *Horn Book Magazine.* Boston: Horn Book.

Rosenberg, B. (1982). *Genreflecting—A guide to reading interests in genre fiction.* Littleton: Libraries Unlimited.

Sims, R. (1979). *Shadow and substance—Afro-American experience in contemporary children's fiction.* Urbana, IL: NCTE.*

Small, R. (Ed.) (1982). *Books for you: A booklist for senior high students.* Urbana IL.: NCTE.*

Standford, B., and Amin, K., (1978). *Black literature for high school students.* Urbana, IL.: NCTE.*

*National Council of Teachers of English, 1111 Kenyon Road, Urbana, IL: 61801.

BIBLIOGRAPHY D

Suggested Books for Secondary Students

The authors and editors listed below are some of the most popular with junior and senior high-school students. Not all titles by each author are listed—just a representative sample from each. The books and poems deal with a wide variety of themes relevant to today's young adults. They are also appropriate for developing thematic units and whole language activities.

Author/Editor	Title
Adoff, Arnold (Ed.)	I Am the Darker Brother: An Anthology of Modern Poems by Negro Americans*
Angell, Judie	Ronnie and Rosey
Angelou, Maya	I Know Why the Caged Bird Sings
	Poems*
	Shaker, Why Don't You Sing?*
	Singin' and Swingin' and Gettin' Merry Like Christmas
Bennett, Jay	The Executioner
Blume, Judy	Are You There God? It's Me, Margaret
	Blubber
	Deenie
	Forever
	It's Not the End of the World
	Then Again, Maybe I Won't
	Tiger Eyes
Bonham, Frank	Cool Cat
	Durango Street
	The Forever Formula
Borland, Hal	When the Legends Die
Bradley, Marion Z.	Mists of Avalon (Darkover series)
Brancato, Robin	Facing Up
	Winning
Bridgers, Sue Ellen	All Together Now
	Home Before Dark
Buchanan, Frank	A Shining Season
Burnford, Sheila	Incredible Journey
Butterworth, William E.	Leroy and the Old Man
	Slaughter by Auto
	Under the Influence
Childress, Alice	A Hero Ain't Nothin' but a Sandwich
	Rainbow Jordan

Cleary, Beverly	*Fifteen*
	Jean and Johnny
Cormier, Robert	*After the First Death*
	I Am the Cheese
	The Chocolate War
Curtis, Edward D.	*The Girl Who Married a Ghost*
Dahl, Roald	*Revolting Rhymes*
	The Giraffe & Pelly and Me
	The Twits
Daly, Maureen	*Seventeenth Summer*
Danzinger, Paula	*Can You Sue Your Parents for Malpractice?*
	The Cat Ate My Gymsuit
	There's a Bat in Bunk Five
Davis, Terry	*Vision Quest*
Duncan, Lois	*Daughters of Eve*
	I Know What You Did Last Summer
	Stranger with My Face
	Summer of Fear
	The Killing of Mr. Griffin
Dunning, S., Lueders, E., & Smith, H. (Eds.)	*Reflections on a Gift of Watermelon Pickle**
	*Some Haystacks Don't Even Have Any Needles**
Eyerly, Jeannette	*Bonnie Jo Go Home*
	Drop-out
Fast, Howard	*April Morning*
Frank, Anne	*The Diary of Anne Frank*
Giovanni, Nikki	*Ego-tripping**
Girion, Barbara	*A Handful of Stars*
	A Tangle of Roots
Golding, William	*Lord of the Flies*
Goldman, William	*The Princess Bride*
	Temple of Gold
Green, Bette	*Morning Is a Long Time Coming*
	Summer of My German Soldier
Greenfield, Eloise	*Honey I Love**
Guest, Judith	*Ordinary People*
Guy, Rosa	*The Disappearance*
	The Friends
Hamilton, Virginia	*Arilla Sun Down*
	M.C. Higgins the Great
	Sweet Whispers, Brother Rush
	The People Could Fly (Ed.)
	Zeely
Hentoff, Nat	*I'm Really Dragged but Nothing Gets Me Down*
	This School Is Driving Me Crazy
Herbert, Frank	*Dune*
	Soul Catcher
Hillerman, Tony	*Dance Hall of the Dead*
	Listening Woman
	The Blessing Way
	The Dark Wind
Hinton, S. E.	*Rumble Fish*
	Tex
	That Was Then, This Is Now
	The Outsiders
Holland, Isabelle	*Dinah and the Green Fat Kingdom*
	Heads You Win, Tails I Lose
	Hitchhike
	Of Love and Death and Other Journeys
	The Man Without a Face

Hughes, Langston	*Selected Poems**
Hughes, Ted	*Season Songs**
	*Under the North Star**
Hunt, Irene	*Across Five Aprils*
	Up a Road Slowly
Janeczko, P.	*Don't Forget to Fly**
Jenkins, Peter	*A Walk Across America/The Walk West*
Jones, Hettie	*The Trees Stand Shining: Poetry of the North American Indian**
Kerr, M. E.	*Dinky Hocker Shoots Smack*
	Gentlehands
	If I Love You, Am I Trapped Forever?
King, Stephen	*Nightshift*
	The Stand
Kingman, Lee	*Head Over Wheels*
	The Peter Pan Bag
Kingston, Maxine Hong	*The Woman Warrior*
Klein, Norma	*It's Not What You Expect*
	It's OK if You Don't Love Me
	Mom, the Wolfman and Me
	Sunshine
Knowles, John	*A Separate Peace*
Knudson, R. R.	*The Zan Series*
	You Are the Rain
Koch, K., and Farell, K.	*Talking to the Sun: An Illustrated Anthology of Poems for Young People**
Lawrence, R. D.	*The North Runner*
Lee, Harper	*To Kill a Mockingbird*
L'Engle, Madeleine	*A Ring of Endless Light*
	A Wrinkle in Time
	The Young Unicorns
LeGuin, Ursula	*The Earthsea Trilogy*
Leslie, Robert	*In the Shadow of a Rainbow*
	The Bears and I
Levenkron, Steven	*The Best Little Girl in the World*
	Kessa
Lewis, C. S.	*The Chronicle of Narnia (series)*
Lipsyte, Robert	*One Fat Summer*
	The Contender
London, Jack	*Call of the Wild*
	White Fang
Lyle, Katie	*Fair Day and Another Step Begun*
	I Will Go Barefoot All Summer for You
McCaffrey, Ann	*Dragonriders of Pern (series)*
	Harper Hall (series)
Mathis, Sharon Bell	*Listen for the Fig Tree*
	Teacup Full of Roses
Mazer, Harry	*Guy Lenny*
	The Island Keeper
	The Last Mission
	The War on Villa Street
Mazer, Norma Fox	*A Figure of Speech*
	Saturday, the Twelfth of October
	Taking Terry Mueller
	Up in Seth's Room
Moore, Lillian	*Think of Shadows**
Mowat, Farley	*The Dog Who Wouldn't Be*
Myers, Walter Dean	*Fast Sam, Cool Clyde and Stuff*
	It Ain't All for Nothin'

	The Golden Serpent
	The Young Landlords
Neihardt, John	*Black Elk Speaks*
Neufeld, John	*A Small Civil War*
	Edgar Allen
	Lisa Bright and Dark
	Sunday Father
O'Dell, Scott	*Island of the Blue Dolphins*
	Sing Down the Moon
O'Neill, Mary	*Hailstones and Halibut Bones**
Peck, Richard	*Are You in the House Alone?*
	Close Enough to Touch
	Dreamland Lake
	Father Figure
	Ghosts I Have Been
	Remembering the Good Times
Peck, Robert Newton	*Fawn*
	The Day No Pigs Would Die
Platt, Kin	*The Boy Who Could Make Himself Disappear*
Rawls, Wilson	*Summer of the Monkeys*
	Where the Red Fern Grows
Salinger, J. D.	*Catcher in the Rye*
Savitz, Harriet	*On the Move*
	The Lionhearted
	Wait Until Tomorrow
Schaefer, Jack	*Shane*
Scoppettone, Sandra	*Chloris and the Creeps*
	Happy Endings Are All Alike
	The Late Great Me
Silverberg, Robert	*Lord Valentine's Castle*
	The Majipoor Chronicles
	Valentine, Pontifex
Silverstein, Shel	*A Light in the Attic**
	*Where the Sidewalk Ends**
Singer, Isaac	*Zlateh the Goat and Other Stories*
Snyder, Anne	*First Step*
	Goodbye, Paper Doll
	My Name Is Davy, I'm an Alcoholic
Stolz, Mary	*Leap Before You Look*
	The Edge of Next Year
Strasser, Todd	*Angel Dust Blues*
	A Very Touchy Subject
	Rock and Roll Nights
Swarthout, Glendon	*Bless the Beasts and Children*
Taylor, Mildred	*Roll of Thunder, Hear My Cry*
Trusky, A. Thomas (Ed.)	*Women Poets of the West: An Anthology, 1850–1950**
Van Allsburg, Chris	*Jumanji*
Walker, Alice	*Goodnight Willie Lee, I'll See You in the Morning**
Walker, Margaret	*Jubilee*
White, Robb	*Deathwatch*
	Up Periscope
Wojciechowska, Maia	*Tuned Out*
Zindel, Bonnie and Paul	*A Star for the Latecomer*
Zindel, Paul	*My Darling, My Hamburger*
	The Pigman
	The Undertaker's Gone Bananas

*Books of poetry